T0222394

Learn Keras for Deep Neural Networks

A Fast-Track Approach to Modern Deep Learning with Python

Jojo Moolayil

Apress®

Learn Keras for Deep Neural Networks

Jojo Moolayil
Vancouver, BC, Canada

ISBN-13 (pbk): 978-1-4842-4239-1 ISBN-13 (electronic): 978-1-4842-4240-7
https://doi.org/10.1007/978-1-4842-4240-7

Library of Congress Control Number: 2018965596

Managing Director, Apress Media LLC: Welmoed Spahr
Acquisitions Editor: Celestin Suresh John
Development Editor: Matthew Moodie
Coordinating Editor: Aditee Mirashi

Cover designed by eStudioCalamar

Cover image designed by Freepik (www.freepik.com)

Distributed to the book trade worldwide by Springer Science+Business Media New York, 233 Spring Street, 6th Floor, New York, NY 10013. Phone 1-800-SPRINGER, fax (201) 348-4505, e-mail orders-ny@springer-sbm.com, or visit www.springeronline.com. Apress Media, LLC is a California LLC and the sole member (owner) is Springer Science + Business Media Finance Inc (SSBM Finance Inc). SSBM Finance Inc is a **Delaware** corporation.

For information on translations, please e-mail rights@apress.com, or visit http://www.apress.com/rights-permissions.

Apress titles may be purchased in bulk for academic, corporate, or promotional use. eBook versions and licenses are also available for most titles. For more information, reference our Print and eBook Bulk Sales web page at http://www.apress.com/bulk-sales.

Any source code or other supplementary material referenced by the author in this book is available to readers on GitHub via the book's product page, located at www.apress.com/978-1-4842-4239-1. For more detailed information, please visit http://www.apress.com/source-code.

Printed on acid-free paper

Table of Contents

About the Author vii

About the Technical Reviewer ix

Acknowledgments xi

Introduction xiii

Chapter 1: An Introduction to Deep Learning and Keras 1

Introduction to DL 1

    Demystifying the Buzzwords 2

    What Are Some Classic Problems Solved by DL in Today's Market? 5

    Decomposing a DL Model 5

Exploring the Popular DL Frameworks 8

    Low-Level DL Frameworks 9

    High-Level DL Frameworks 11

A Sneak Peek into the Keras Framework 13

    Getting the Data Ready 15

    Defining the Model Structure 15

    Training the Model and Making Predictions 15

Summary 16

Chapter 2: Keras in Action 17

Setting Up the Environment 17

    Selecting the Python Version 17

    Installing Python for Windows, Linux, or macOS 18

    Installing Keras and TensorFlow Back End 19

Getting Started with DL in Keras...21

    Input Data...21

    Neuron..23

    Activation Function...24

    Sigmoid Activation Function...25

    Model...28

    Layers..28

    The Loss Function 32

    Optimizers 35

    Metrics 39

    Model Configuration 39

    Model Training 40

    Model Evaluation 43

Putting All the Building Blocks Together 45

Summary..52

Chapter 3: Deep Neural Networks for Supervised Learning: Regression...53

Getting Started...53

Problem Statement 55

    Why Is Representing a Problem Statement with a Design Principle Important?...56

    Designing an SCQ..57

    Designing the Solution 59

Exploring the Data..60

    Looking at the Data Dictionary 63

    Finding Data Types 66

    Working with Time..67

    Predicting Sales...69

Exploring Numeric Columns 70

Understanding the Categorical Features 74

Data Engineering 78

Defining Model Baseline Performance 84

Designing the DNN 85

Testing the Model Performance 89

Improving the Model 89

Increasing the Number of Neurons 93

Plotting the Loss Metric Across Epochs 97

Testing the Model Manually 98

Summary 99

Chapter 4: Deep Neural Networks for Supervised Learning: Classification 101

Getting Started 101

Problem Statement 102

Designing the SCQ 103

Designing the Solution 103

Exploring the Data 104

Data Engineering 110

Defining Model Baseline Accuracy 118

Designing the DNN for Classification 119

Revisiting the Data 124

Standardize, Normalize, or Scale the Data 124

Transforming the Input Data 126

DNNs for Classification with Improved Data 127

Summary 134

Chapter 5: Tuning and Deploying Deep Neural Networks 137

The Problem of Overfitting 137

So, What Is Regularization? 139

L1 Regularization 140

L2 Regularization 140

Dropout Regularization 141

Hyperparameter Tuning 142

Hyperparameters in DL 143

Approaches for Hyperparameter Tuning 147

Model Deployment 152

Tailoring the Test Data 152

Saving Models to Memory 154

Retraining the Models with New Data 155

Online Models 156

Delivering Your Model As an API 157

Putting All the Pieces of the Puzzle Together 158

Summary 159

Chapter 6: The Path Ahead 161

What's Next for DL Expertise? 161

CNN 162

RNN 167

CNN + RNN 170

Why Do We Need GPU for DL? 171

Other Hot Areas in DL (GAN) 174

Concluding Thoughts 176

Index 177

About the Author

Jojo Moolayil is an artificial intelligence, deep learning, machine learning, and decision science professional and the author of the book *Smarter Decisions: The Intersection of IoT and Decision Science* (Packt, 2016). He has worked with industry leaders on several high-impact and critical data science and machine learning projects across multiple verticals. He is currently associated with Amazon Web Services as a Research Scientist–AI.

Jojo was born and raised in Pune, India and graduated from the University of Pune with a major in Information Technology Engineering. He started his career with Mu Sigma Inc., the world's largest pure-play analytics provider, and worked with the leaders of many Fortune 50 clients. He later worked with Flutura, an IoT analytics startup, and GE, the pioneer and leader in industrial AI.

He currently resides in Vancouver, BC. Apart from authoring books on deep learning, decision science, and IoT, Jojo has also been technical reviewer for various books on the same subject with Apress and Packt Publishing. He is an active data science tutor and maintains a blog at http://blog.jojomoolayil.com.

Jojo's personal website: www.jojomoolayil.com
Business e-mail: mail@jojomoolayil.com

About the Technical Reviewer

Manohar Swamynathan is a data science practitioner and an avid programmer, with over 13 years of experience in various data science–related areas that include data warehousing, business intelligence (BI), analytical tool development, ad hoc analysis, predictive modeling, data science product development, consulting, formulating strategy, and executing analytics programs. He's had a career covering the life cycles of data across different domains such as US mortgage banking, retail/e-commerce, insurance, and industrial IoT. He has a bachelor's degree with a specialization in physics, mathematics, and computers, and a master's degree in project management. He currently lives in Bengaluru, the Silicon Valley of India.

He has authored the book *Mastering Machine Learning with Python in Six Steps* (Apress, 2017). You can learn more about his various other activities on his website, http://www.mswamynathan.com.

Acknowledgments

I would like to thank my parents, my brother Tijo, and my sister Josna for their constant support and love.

Introduction

This book is intended to gear the readers with a superfast crash course on deep learning. Readers are expected to have basic programming skills in any modern-day language; Python experience would be great, but is not necessary. Given the limitations on the size and depth of the subject we can cover, this short guide is intended to equip you as a beginner with sound understanding of the topic, including tangible practical experience in model development that will help develop a foundation in the deep learning domain.

This guide is not recommended if you are already above the beginner level and are keen to explore advanced topics in deep learning like computer vision, speech recognition, and so on. The topics of CNN, RNN, and modern unsupervised learning algorithms are beyond the scope of this guide. We provide only a brief introduction to these to keep the readers aware contextually about more advanced topics and also provide recommended sources to explore these topics in more detail.

What will you learn from this guide?

The book is focused on a fast-paced approach to exploring practical deep learning concepts with math and programming-friendly abstractions. You will learn to design, develop, train, validate, and deploy deep neural networks using the industry's favorite Keras framework. You will also learn about the best practices for debugging and validating deep learning models and briefly learn about deploying and integrating deep learning as a service into a larger software service or product. Finally, with the experience gained in building deep learning models with Keras, you will also be able to extend the same principles into other popular frameworks.

Who is this book for?

The primary target audience for this book consists of software engineers and data engineers keen on exploring deep learning for a career move or an upcoming enterprise tech project. We understand the time crunch you may be under and the pain of assimilating new content to get started with the least amount of friction. Additionally, this book is for data science enthusiasts and academic and research professionals exploring deep learning as a tool for research and experiments.

What is the approach to learning in the book?

We follow the lazy programming approach in this guide. We start with a basic introduction, and then cater to the required context incrementally at each step. We discuss how each building block functions in a lucid way and then learn about the abstractions available to implement them.

How is the book structured?

The book is organized into three sections with two chapters each.

Section 1 equips you with all the necessary gear to get started on the fast-track ride into deep learning. Chapter 1 introduces the topic of deep learning, details its differences from similar fields, and explores the choices of frameworks for deep learning with a deeper look at the Keras ecosystem. Chapter 2 will help you get started with a hands-on exercise in Keras, understanding the basic building blocks of deep learning and developing the first basic DNN.

Section 2 embraces the fundamentals of deep learning in simple, lucid language while abstracting the math and complexities of model training and validation with the least amount of code without compromising on flexibility, scale, and the required sophistication. Chapter 3 explores a business problem that can be solved by supervised learning algorithms with deep neural networks. We tackle one use case for regression and another for classification, leveraging popular Kaggle datasets. Chapter 4 delves into the craft of validating deep neural networks (i.e., measuring performance and understanding the shortcomings and the means to circumvent them).

Section 3 concludes the book with topics on further model improvement and the path forward. Chapter 5 discusses an interesting and challenging part of deep learning (i.e., hyperparameter tuning). Finally, Chapter 6—the conclusion—discusses the path ahead for the reader to further hone his or her skills in deep learning and discusses a few areas of active development and research in deep learning.

At the end of this crash course, the reader will have gained a thorough understanding of the deep learning principles within the shortest possible time frame and will have obtained practical hands-on experience in developing enterprise-grade deep learning solutions in Keras.

CHAPTER 1

An Introduction to Deep Learning and Keras

In this chapter, we will explore the field of deep learning (DL) with a brief introduction and then move to have a look at the popular choices of available frameworks for DL development. We will also take a closer look at the Keras ecosystem to understand why it is special and have a look at a sample code to understand how easy the framework is for developing DL models.

Let's get started.

Introduction to DL

We'll first start with a formal definition and then tackle a simple way of delineating the topic.

> *DL is a subfield of machine learning (ML) in artificial intelligence (AI) that deals with algorithms inspired from the biological structure and functioning of a brain to aid machines with intelligence.*

© Jojo Moolayil 2019
J. Moolayil, *Learn Keras for Deep Neural Networks*,
https://doi.org/10.1007/978-1-4842-4240-7_1

Maybe this was too high level or probably difficult to consume, so let's break it down step by step. We see three important terms in the definition, in a specific order: DL, ML, and AI. Let's first tackle these buzzwords individually, starting with AI.

Demystifying the Buzzwords

AI in its most generic form can be defined as the quality of intelligence being introduced into machines. Machines are usually dumb, so to make them smarter we induce some sort of intelligence in them where they can take a decision independently. One example would be a washing machine that can decide on the right amount of water to use and on the required time for soaking, washing, and spinning; that is, it makes a decision when specific inputs are provided and therefore works in a smarter way. Similarly, an ATM could make a call on disbursing the amount you want with the right combination of notes available in the machine. This intelligence is technically induced in the machine in an artificial way, thus the name AI.

Another point to note is that the intelligence here is explicitly programmed, say a comprehensive list of if-else rules . The engineer who designed the system carefully thought through all the combinations possible and designed a rule-based system that can make decisions by traversing through the defined rule path. What if we need to introduce intelligence in a machine without explicit programming, probably something where the machine can learn on its own? That's when we touch base with ML.

> *Machine learning can be defined as the process of inducing intelligence into a system or machine without explicit programming.*
>
> —Andrew NG, Stanford Adjunct Professor

Examples for ML could be a system that could predict whether a student will fail or pass in a test by learning from the historical test results and student attributes. Here, the system is not encoded with a comprehensive list of all possible rules that can decide whether a student will pass or fail; instead, the system learns on its own based on the patterns it learned from the historical data.

So, where does DL stand within this context? It happens that while ML works very well for a variety of problems, it fails to excel in some specific cases that seem to be very easy for humans: say, classifying an image as a cat or dog, distinguishing an audio clip as of a male or female voice, and so on. ML performs poorly with image and other unstructured data types. Upon researching the reasons for this poor performance, an inspiration led to the idea of mimicking the human brain's biological process, which is composed of billions of neurons connected and orchestrated to adapt to learning new things. On a parallel track, neural networks had already been a research topic for several years, but only limited progress had been made due to the computational and data limitations at the time. When researchers reached the cusp of ML and neural networks, there came the field of DL, which was framed by developing deep neural networks (DNNs), that is, improvised neural networks with many more layers. DL excelled at the new frontiers where ML was falling behind. In due course, additional research and experimentation led to the understanding of where we could leverage DL for all ML tasks and expect better performance, provided there was surplus data availability. DL, therefore, became a ubiquitous field to solve predictive problems rather than just being confined to areas of computer vision, speech, and so on.

Today, we can leverage DL for almost all use cases that were earlier solved using ML and expect to outperform our previous achievements, provided that there is a surplus of data. This realization has led to distinguishing the order of the fields based on data. A new rule of thumb was established: ML would not be able to improve performance with increased training data after a certain threshold, whereas DL was able to leverage the surplus data more effectively for improved performance. The same was true a few years back in the debate between statistical models and ML. The following chart is an illustration to represent the overall idea of model performance with data size for the three aforementioned fields.

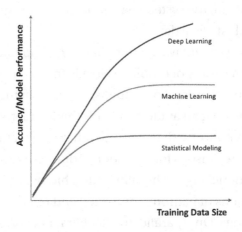

Now, if we revisit the formal definition, you can probably make a better sense of the statement that the AI subfield of ML is inspired by the biological aspects of a human brain. We can simplify the three fields using a simple Venn diagram, as shown in the following.

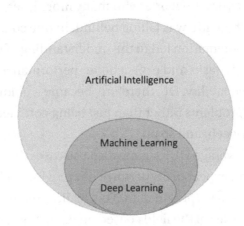

Putting it all together, we can say that AI is the field of inducing intelligence into a machine or system artificially, with or without explicit programming. ML is a subfield in AI where intelligence is induced without explicit programming. Lastly, DL is a field within ML where intelligence is induced into systems without explicit programming using algorithms that have been inspired by the biological functioning of the human brain.

What Are Some Classic Problems Solved by DL in Today's Market?

Today, we can see the adoption of DL in a variety of day-to-day aspects of our life in the digital world. If you are active on social media, you might have noticed Facebook suggesting tagging your friends when you upload a picture. Also note the self-driving mode in Tesla's cars, predictions of the next word in the messaging system on your iOS or Android phone, Alexa, Siri, and Google Assistant responding to you as a human, and so on. If we try to analyze the type of use cases we can solve using DL, we can already witness the power of DL in almost any system you use in today's world.

Decomposing a DL Model

In its most basic form, DL models are designed using neural network architecture. A neural network is a hierarchical organization of neurons (similar to the neurons in the brain) with connections to other neurons. These neurons pass a message or signal to other neurons based on the received input and form a complex network that learns with some feedback mechanism.

The following is a simplistic representation of a basic neural network.

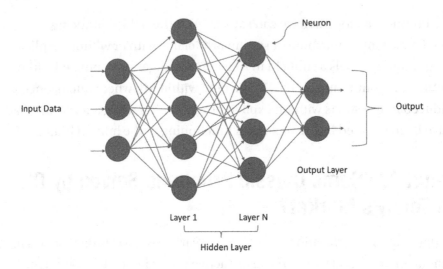

As you can see in the preceding figure, the input data is consumed by the neurons in the first hidden layer, which then provides an output to the next layer and so on, eventually resulting in the final output. Each layer can have one or many neurons, and each of them will compute a small function (e.g., activation function). The connection between two neurons of successive layers would have an associated weight. The weight defines the influence of the input to the output for the next neuron and eventually for the overall final output. In a neural network, the initial weights would all be random during the model training, but these weights are updated iteratively to learn to predict a correct output. Decomposing the network, we can define few logical building blocks like neuron, layer, weight, input, output, an activation function inside the neuron to compute a learning process, and so on.

For an intuitive understanding, let's take an example of how a human brain learns to identify different people. When you meet a person for the second time, you will be able to identify him. How does this happen? People have a resemblance in overall structure; two eyes, two ears, a nose, lips, and so on. Everyone has the same structure, yet we are able to distinguish between people quite easily, right?

The nature of the learning process in the brain is quite intuitive. Rather than learning the structure of the face to identify people, the brain learns the deviation from a generic face (e.g., how different an individual's eyes are from the reference eye), which can then be quantified as an electrical signal with a defined strength. Similarly, it learns deviations from all parts of the face from a reference base, combines these deviations into new dimensions, and finally gives an output. All of this happens so quickly that none of us realizes what our subconscious mind has actually done.

Similarly, the neural network showcased in the preceding illustration tries to mimic the same process using a mathematical approach. The input is consumed by neurons in the first layer and an activation function is calculated within each neuron. Based on a simple rule, it forwards an output to the next neuron, similar to the deviations learned by the human brain. The larger the output of a neuron, the larger the significance of that input dimension will be. These dimensions are then combined in the next layer to form additional new dimensions, which we probably can't make sense of. But the system learns it intuitively. The process, when multiplied several times, develops a complex network with several connections.

Now that the structure of the neural network is understood, let's understand how the learning happens. When we provide the input data to the defined structure, the end output would be a prediction, which could be either correct or incorrect. Based on the output, if we provide a feedback to the network to adapt better by using some means to make a better prediction, the system learns by updating the weight for the connections. To achieve the process of providing feedback and defining the next step to make changes in the correct way, we use a beautiful mathematical algorithm called "backpropagation." Iterating the process several times step by step, with more and more data, helps the network update the weights appropriately to create a system where it can make a decision for predicting output based on the rules it has created for itself through the weights and connections.

The name "deep neural networks" evolved from the use of many more hidden layers, making it a "deep" network to learn more complex patterns. The success stories of DL have only surfaced in the last few years because the process of training a network is computationally heavy and needs large amounts of data. The experiments finally saw the light of the day only when computer and data storage became more available and affordable.

Exploring the Popular DL Frameworks

Given that the adoption of DL has proceeded at an alarming pace, the maturity of the ecosystem has also shown phenomenal improvement. Thanks to many large tech organizations and open source initiatives, we now have a plethora of options to choose from. Before we delve into the specifics of various frameworks, let us understand why would we essentially need a framework and what could be used as an alternative.

Let's start by understanding how the software industry evolved in frameworks.

If you observe the evolution of the software industry, you will understand that today it is far easier to develop high-end software than it was a few years back. Credit for this goes to the available tools that have automated or abstracted complex problems in a way that's simple use. The tech-fraternity has been benevolent and innovative in contributing great ideas. We build new services that are built on top of the previous ones and will ultimately create a complex service that will be capable of orchestrating the collection of services while being secure as well as scalable. Given the maturity of software tools available today, we can afford to abstract several complexities that happen in the background. These tools are nothing but building blocks for software systems. You technically don't need to start from scratch; you can instead rely on available powerful tools that have matured significantly to take care of several software-building services.

Similarly, in DL, there are a set of code blocks that can be reused for different types of use cases. The same algorithm with a different parameter value can be used for a different use case, so why not package the algorithm as a simple function or a class? Several aspects of DL have been developed as reusable codes that can today be directly used from frameworks that do an excellent job of abstracting the idea. Building blocks in a DL model include the neurons, activation functions, optimization algorithms, data augmentation tools, and so on. You could indeed develop a DNN from scratch, say in C++, Java, or Python, with ~1000 lines of code, or probably use a framework and reuse available tools with maybe 10–15 lines of code. That being said, let's have a look at the popular choices of DL frameworks used in the industry today.

Low-Level DL Frameworks

Given the level of abstraction a framework provides, we can classify it as a low-level or high-level DL framework. While this is by no means industry-recognized terminology, we can use this segregation for a more intuitive understanding of the frameworks. The following are a few of the popular low-level frameworks for DL.

Theano

Theano was one of the first DL libraries to gain popularity. It was developed by the Montreal Institute for Learning Algorithms (MILA) at the University of Montreal. Theano is an open source Python library that was made available in 2007; the last main release was published in late 2017 by MILA.

Additional details are available at

```
http://deeplearning.net/software/theano/

https://github.com/Theano/Theano/
```

Torch

Torch is another popular ML and DL framework based on the Lua programming language. It was initially developed by Ronan Collobert, Koray Kavukcuoglu, and Clement Farabet but was later improved by Facebook with a set of extension modules as open source software.

Additional details are available at

```
http://torch.ch/
```

PyTorch

PyTorch is an open source ML and DL library for Python and was developed by the Facebook AI research team. PyTorch has become more popular than Torch, since anyone with a basic understanding of Python can get started on developing DL models. Moreover, PyTorch was far easier and transparent to use for DL development.

Additional details are available at

```
https://pytorch.org/
```

MxNet

Pronounced "mix-net," MxNet stands for both "mix" and "maximize" and was developed by researchers from CMU, NYU, NUS, MIT, and others. The idea was simplified to combine declarative and imperative programming together (mix) to maximize efficiency and productivity. It supports the use of multiple GPUs and is widely supported by major cloud providers like AWS and Azure.

Additional details are available at

```
https://mxnet.apache.org/
```

TensorFlow

TensorFlow is undoubtedly one of the most popular and widely used DL frameworks in the DL fraternity. It was developed and open sourced by Google and supports deployment across CPUs, GPUs, and mobile and edge devices as well. It was released in November 2015 and then saw a huge increase in its adoption within the industry.

> www.tensorflow.org/

The list of DL frameworks is a long one, and discussing all of them is beyond the scope of our book. A few other popular frameworks you could additionally research are Caffe, Microsoft CNTK, Chainer, PaddlePaddle, and so on. Discussing the pros and cons of one framework over other is another interesting and never-ending debate. I would highly recommend that you explore and understand what improvements each framework has to offer.

This would be a good starting point:

> https://blogs.technet.microsoft.com/
> machinelearning/2018/03/14/comparing-deep-
> learning-frameworks-a-rosetta-stone-approach/

High-Level DL Frameworks

The previously mentioned frameworks can be defined as the first level of abstraction for DL models. You would still need to write fairly long codes and scripts to get your DL model ready, although much less so than using just Python or C++. The advantage of using the first-level abstraction is the flexibility it provides in designing a model.

However, to simplify the process of DL models, we have frameworks that work on the second level of abstraction; that is, rather than using the previously mentioned frameworks directly, we can use a new framework on top of an existing framework and thereby simplify DL model development even further.

11

The most popular high-level DL framework that provides a second-level abstraction to DL model development is Keras. Other frameworks like Gluon, Lasagne, and so on are also available, but Keras has been the most widely adopted one.

Note   While Gluon works on top of MxNet, and Lasagne on top of Theano, Keras can work on top of TensorFlow, Theano, MxNet, and Microsoft CNTK. The list has been aggressively expanding, and quite possibly by the time you read this book many more will have been added.

Keras is a high-level neural network API written in Python and can help you in developing a fully functional DL model with less than 15 lines of code. Since it is written in Python, it has a larger community of users and supporters and is extremely easy to get started with. The simplicity of Keras is that it helps users quickly develop DL models and provides a ton of flexibility while still being a high-level API. This really makes Keras a special framework to work with. Moreover, given that it supports several other frameworks as a back end, it adds the flexibility to leverage a different low-level API for a different use case if required. By far the most widely adopted usage of Keras is with TensorFlow as a back end (i.e., Keras as a high-level DL API and TensorFlow as its low-level API back end). In a nutshell, the code you write in Keras gets converted to TensorFlow, which then runs on a compute instance.

You can read more about Keras and its recent developments here:

https://keras.io/

A Sneak Peek into the Keras Framework

Now that we have an understanding of the different frameworks available for DL as well as the need to use one of them, we can take a sneak peek into why Keras has an unfair advantage in DL development before we conclude the chapter. We will definitely take a deeper look at what Keras has to offer in the next chapter, but it is interesting to look at the beauty of Keras in action before we end this chapter.

Have a look at the DNN showcased in the following.

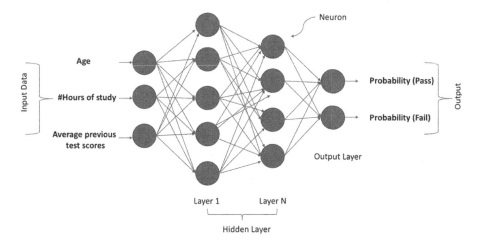

Yes, this is the same figure we saw earlier while exploring the topic "Decomposing a DL Model." If we try to define the network, we can say that it is a DNN that has two hidden layers with five and four neurons, respectively. The first hidden layer accepts an input data that has three dimensions and gives an output in the output layer with two neurons.

To have this make more intuitive sense, we can assume that this is a simple DNN for a problem like predicting whether a student will pass or fail based on some input data.

Say we have the age, the number of hours studied, and the average score out of 100 for all the previous tests for which he appeared as the input data point.

Building a neural network in Keras is as simple as the following script. It is absolutely fine not to understand the whole code that follows at the moment; we will explore this step by step in more detail in the next chapter.

```
#Import required packages
from keras.models import Sequential
from keras.layers import Dense
import numpy as np

# Getting the data ready
# Generate train dummy data for 1000 Students and dummy test
for 500
#Columns :Age, Hours of Study &Avg Previous test scores
np.random.seed(2018). #Setting seed for reproducibility
train_data, test_data = np.random.random((1000, 3)), np.random.
random((500, 3))
#Generate dummy results for 1000 students : Whether Passed (1)
or Failed (0)
labels = np.random.randint(2, size=(1000, 1))

#Defining the model structure with the required layers, # of
neurons, activation function and optimizers
model = Sequential()
model.add(Dense(5, input_dim=3, activation='relu'))
model.add(Dense(4, activation='relu'))
model.add(Dense(1, activation='sigmoid'))
model.compile(loss='binary_crossentropy', optimizer='adam',
metrics=['accuracy'])
```

```
#Train the model and make predictions
model.fit(train_data, labels, epochs=10, batch_size=32)
#Make predictions from the trained model
predictions = model.predict(test_data)
```

The preceding code can be divided into three sections.

Getting the Data Ready

Normally, we would spend some time with the data by importing and exploring the content and making necessary augmentations to the data as the model's input. Here, since this is a dummy use case, we are just using a random number generator in Python's numpy package to create a dummy training dataset for 1000 students, another dummy test dataset for 500 students, and lastly, the labels or actual outputs for the students (i.e., whether they passed or failed).

Defining the Model Structure

Once we have the data ready in the necessary format, we would need to first design the structure of the DNN. We define the number and types of layers, the number of neurons in each layer, the required activation function, the optimizer to use, and few other network attributes.

Training the Model and Making Predictions

Once the network is defined, we can use the training data with the correct predictions to train the network using the "fit" method for the model. Finally, once the model is trained, we can use the trained model to make predictions on the new test dataset.

I hope this example, though oversimplified, will give you an understanding of how easy it to use the Keras framework to develop DL models. If understanding the code was overwhelming at this point, it's absolutely fine. We will tackle codes step by step in detail in the next chapter.

Summary

In this chapter, we have learned the basics of DL with a simple introduction and also explored a few examples of common use cases that leverage DL in our day-to-day digital lives. We then studied the need for using a DL framework for developing models and explored a few low-level as well as high-level frameworks available in the industry. We then looked at Keras, our preferred framework for this book, with a simple dummy example in order to see the simplicity of creating DL models.

In the next chapter, we will take a deeper look at Keras and the various building blocks it offers. We will try developing a simple DL model with hands-on exercises using Keras and Python.

CHAPTER 2

Keras in Action

In this chapter, we will explore the Keras framework and get started with hands-on exercises to learn the basics of Keras along with a bit of Python and the necessary DL topics. A word of caution, given that this a fast-track guide: we will not have the scope to talk in detail about exhaustive topics in DL. Instead, we will start with a simple topic, explore the basic idea behind it, and add references where you can dive deeper for a more foundational understanding of the topic.

Setting Up the Environment

As discussed earlier, we will be developing DL models with the Keras stack using TensorFlow as a back end in Python. Hence, to get started we need to set up our playground environment by installing Python, a few important Python packages, TensorFlow, and finally Keras.

Let's get started.

Selecting the Python Version

Python is currently available in two major versions: 2.7.x and 3.x. Although Python 3.x is the most recent version and the future of Python, there have been a series of conflicts due to backward incapability in the developer community with regard to the transition from 2.7 to 3.x. Unfortunately, many developers are still connected with the Python 2.7.x version.

© Jojo Moolayil 2019
J. Moolayil, *Learn Keras for Deep Neural Networks*,
https://doi.org/10.1007/978-1-4842-4240-7_2

However, for our use case, I highly recommend getting started with Python 3.x, given that it is the future. Some may be reluctant to start with Python 3, assuming there will be issues with many packages in the 3.x version, but for almost all practical use cases, we have all major DL, ML, and other useful packages already updated for 3.x.

Installing Python for Windows, Linux, or macOS

There are many distributions of Python available in the market. You could either download and install Python from the official python.org website or choose any popular distribution. For ML and DL, the most recommended distribution of Python is the Anaconda distribution from Continuum Analytics. Anaconda is a free and open source distribution of Python, especially for ML and DL large-scale processing. It simplifies the entire package management and deployment process and comes with a very easy to use virtual environment manager and a couple of additional tools for coding like Jupyter Notebooks and the Spyder IDE.

To get started with Anaconda, you can go to `www.anaconda.com/download/` and select an appropriate version based on the OS (Mac/Windows/Linux) and architecture (32 bit/64 bit) of your choice. At the time of writing this book, the most recent version of Python 3 is 3.6. By the time you read this book, there might be a newer version available. You should comfortably download and install the most updated version of Anaconda Python.

Once you have downloaded the installer, please install the application.

For Windows users, this will be a simple executable file installation. Double-click the .exe file downloaded from Anaconda's website and follow the visual onscreen guidelines to complete the installation process.

Linux users can use the following command after navigating to the downloaded folder:

```
bash Anaconda-latest-Linux-x86_64.sh
```

Mac users can install the software by double-clicking the downloaded .pkg file and then following the onscreen instructions.

The Anaconda distribution of Python eases out the process for DL and ML by installing all major Python packages required for DL.

Installing Keras and TensorFlow Back End

Now that Python is set up, we need to install TensorFlow and Keras. Installing packages in Python can be done easily using the `pip`, a package manager for Python. You can install any Python package with the command `pip install package-name` in the terminal or command prompt.

So, let's install our required packages (i.e., TensorFlow and Keras).

```
pip install keras
```

followed by

```
pip install tensorflow
```

In case you face any issues in setting Anaconda Python with TensorFlow and Keras, or you want to experiment only within a Python virtual environment, you can explore a more detailed installation guide here:

```
https://medium.com/@margaretmz/anaconda-jupyter-notebook-
tensorflow-and-keras-b91f381405f8
```

Also, you might want to install TensorFlow with GPU support if your system has any NVIDIA CUDA–compatible GPUs. Here is a link to a step-by-step guide to install TensorFlow with GPU support on Windows, Mac and Linux:

```
www.tensorflow.org/install/
```

To check if your GPU is CUDA compatible, please explore the list available on NVIDIA's official website:

```
https://developer.nvidia.com/cuda-gpus
```

To write codes and develop models, you can choose the IDE provided by Anaconda (i.e., Spyder), the native terminal or command prompt, or a web-based notebook IDE called Jupyter Notebooks. For all data science–related experiments, I would highly recommend using Jupyter Notebooks for the convenience it provides in exploratory analysis and reproducibility. We will be using Jupyter Notebooks for all experiments in our book.

Jupyter Notebooks comes preinstalled with Anaconda Python; in case you are using a virtual environment, you might have to install it using the package manager or just the command

```
conda install jupyter
```

To start Jupyter Notebooks, you can use the Anaconda Navigator or just enter the command

```
jupyter notebook
```

inside your command prompt or terminal; then, Jupyter should start in your default browser on localhost. The following screenshot shows when Jupyter is running in the browser.

Click the 'New' button at the extreme right and select Python from the drop-down menu. If you have installed one or more virtual environments, all of them will show up in the drop-down; please select the Python environment of your choice.

Once selected, your Jupyter notebook should open and should be ready to get started. The following screenshot showcases a Jupyter notebook up and running in the browser.

The green highlighted cell is where you write your code, and Ctrl + Enter will execute the selected cell. You can add more cells with the '+' icon in the control bar or explore additional options from the Menu bar. If this is your first time with Jupyter, I recommend the available options in the navigation menu.

Now that we have all the required tools set up and running, let's start with simple DL building blocks with Keras.

Getting Started with DL in Keras

Let's start by studying the DNN and its logical components, understanding what each component is used for and how these building blocks are mapped in the Keras framework.

If you recall the topic "Decomposing a DL Model" from Chapter 1, we had defined the logical components in a DNN as input data, neurons, activation functions, layer (i.e., group of neurons), connections between neurons or edges, a learning procedure (i.e., the backpropagation algorithm), and the output layer.

Let's look at at these logical components one by one.

Input Data

Input data for a DL algorithm can be of a variety of types. Essentially, the model understands data as "tensors". Tensors are nothing but a generic form for vectors, or in computer engineering terms, a simple n-dimensional matrix. Data of any form is finally represented as a homogeneous numeric matrix. So, if the data is tabular, it will be a two-dimensional tensor where each column represents one training sample and the entire table/matrix will be m samples. To understand this better, have a look at the following visual illustration.

2 dimensional tensor with shape (m x n)

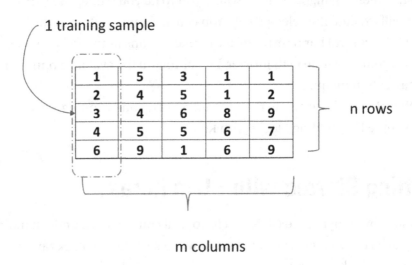

1 training sample

n rows

m columns

You could also reverse the representation of training samples (i.e., each row could be one training sample), so in the context of the student passing/failing in the test example, one row would indicate all the attributes of one student (his marks, age, etc.). And for n rows, we would have a dataset with n training samples. But in DL experiments, it is common notation to use one training sample in a column. Thus, m columns would denote m samples.

Additionally, DL models can interpret only numeric data. If the dataset has any categorical data like "gender" with values of "male" and "female," we will need to convert them to one-hot encoded variables (i.e., simply representing the columns with a value of 0 or 1, where 0 would represent "male" and 1 would represent "female" or vice versa).

Image data also needs to be transformed into an n-dimensional tensor. We will not cover DL models for image data in this book but I do want to keep you aware of its representation as input data. An image is stored in data as a three-dimensional tensor where two dimensions define the pixel values on a 2D plane and a third dimension defines the values for RGB color channels. So essentially, one image becomes a three-dimensional tensor and n images will be a four-dimensional tensor, where the fourth dimension will stack a 3D tensor image as a training sample. Therefore, if we have 100 images with a 512×512-pixel resolution, they will be represented as a 4D tensor with shape $512 \times 512 \times 3 \times 100$.

Lastly, it is a good practice to normalize, standardize, or scale the input values before training. Normalizing the values will bring all values in the input tensor into a 0–1 range, and standardization will bring the values into a range where the mean is 0 and the standard deviation is 1. This helps to reduce computation, as the learning improves by a great margin and so does performance, as the activation functions (covered in the following) behave more appropriately.

Neuron

At the core of the DNN, we have neurons where computation for an output is executed. A neuron receives one or more inputs from the neurons in the previous layer. If the neurons are in the first hidden layer, they will receive the data from the input data stream. In the biological neuron, an electric signal is given as an output when it receives an input with a higher influence. To map that functionality in the mathematical neuron, we need to have a function that operates on the sum of input multiplied by the corresponding weights (denoted as $f(z)$ in the following visual) and responds with an appropriate value based on the input. If a higher-influence input is received, the output should be higher, and vice versa. It is in a way analogous to the activation signal (i.e., higher influence -> then activate, otherwise deactivate). The function that works on the computed input data is called the activation function.

A Single Neuron

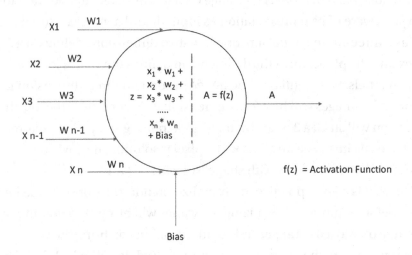

Activation Function

An activation function is the function that takes the combined input z as shown in the preceding illustration, applies a function on it, and passes the output value, thus trying to mimic the activate/deactivate function. The activation function, therefore, determines the state of a neuron by computing the activation function on the combined input.

A quick thought crossing your mind might be as follows: why do we really need an activation function to compute the combined output z, when we could just pass the value of z as the final output? There are several problems here. Firstly, the range of the output value would be -Infinity to + Infinity, where we won't have a clear way of defining a threshold where activation should happen. Secondly, the network will in a way be rendered useless, as it won't really learn. This is where a bit of calculus and derivatives come into the picture. To simplify the story, we can say that if your activation function is a linear function (basically no activation), then the derivative of that function becomes 0; this becomes a big issue because training with the backpropagation algorithm helps give feedback to the network about wrong classifications and thereby helps a neuron to adjust its weights by using a derivative of the function. If that becomes 0, the network loses out on this learning ability. To put it another way, we can say there is really no point of having the DNN, as the output of having just one layer would be similar to having n layers. To keep things simple, we would always need a nonlinear activation function (at least in all hidden layers) to get the network to learn properly.

There are a variety of choices available to use as an activation function. The most common ones are the sigmoid function and the ReLU (rectified linear unit).

Sigmoid Activation Function

A sigmoid function is defined as $\dfrac{1}{\left(1+e^{-z}\right)}$, which renders the output between 0 and 1 as shown in the following illustration. The nonlinear output (s shaped as shown) improves the learning process very well, as it closely resembles the following principle—*lower influence: low output* and *higher influence: higher output*—and also confines the output within the 0-to-1 range.

In Keras, the sigmoid activation function is available as keras. activations.sigmoid(x).

We can import this into Python simply with the `import` command:

```
import keras.activations.sigmoid
```

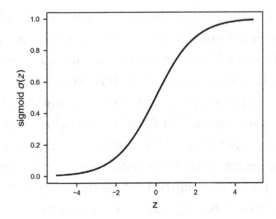

ReLU Activation Function

Similarly, the ReLU uses the function **f(z) = max(0,z),** which means that if the output is positive it would output the same value, otherwise it would output 0. The function's output range is shown in the following visual.

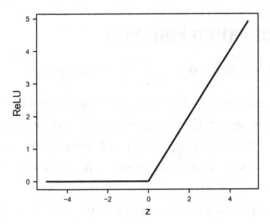

Keras provides ReLU as

```
keras.activations.relu(x, alpha=0.0, max_value=None)
```

The function may look linear, but it isn't. ReLU is a valid nonlinear function and in fact works really well as an activation function. It not only improves the performance but significantly helps the number of computations to be reduced during the training phase. This is a direct result of the 0 value in the output when z is negative, thereby deactivating the neuron.

But because of the horizontal line with 0 as the output, we can face serious issues sometimes. For instance, in the previous section we discussed a horizontal line, which is a constant with a derivative of 0 and therefore may become a bottleneck during training, as the weights will not easily get updated. To circumvent the problem, there was a new activation function proposed: Leaky ReLU, where the negative value outputs a slightly slanting line instead of a horizontal line, which helps in updating the weights through backpropagation effectively.

Leaky ReLU is defined as

$f(z) = z$; when z >0

$f(z) = \alpha z$; when z<0 and where α is a parameter that is defined as a small constant, say 0.005

Keras provides Leaky ReLU as follows:

```
keras.layers.LeakyReLU(X, alpha=0.0, max_value=None).
```

We can directly use the activation function by setting the value of alpha with a small constant.

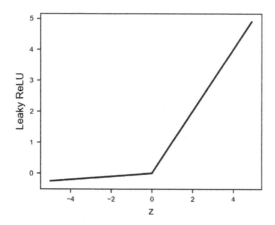

There are many more activation functions that can be used in a DNN and are available in Keras. A few other popular ones are tanh (hyperbolic tan activation), swish activation, elu (exponential linear unit), selu (scaled elu), and so on.

Model

The overall structure of a DNN is developed using the model object in Keras. This provides a simple way to create a stack of layers by adding new layers one after the other.

The easiest way to define a model is by using the sequential model, which allows easy creation of a linear stack of layers.

The following example showcases the creation of a simple sequential model with one layer followed by an activation. The layer would have 10 neurons and would receive an input with 15 neurons and be activated with the ReLU activation function.

```
from keras.models import Sequential
from keras.layers import Dense, Activation

model = Sequential()
model.add(Dense(10, input_dim=15))
model.add(Activation('relu'))
```

Layers

A layer in the DNN is defined as a group of neurons or a logically separated group in a hierarchical network structure. As DL became more and more popular, there were several experiments conducted with network architectures to improve performance for a variety of use cases. The use cases centered around regular supervised algorithms like classification and regression, computer vision experiments, extending DL for natural language processing and understanding, speech recognition, and combinations of different domains. To simplify the model development process, Keras provides us with several types of layers and various means to connect them. Discussing all of them would be beyond the scope of the book. However, we will take a close look at a few layers and also glance through some important layers for other advanced use cases, which you can explore later.

Core Layers

There are a few important layers that we will be using in most use cases.

Dense Layer

A dense layer is a regular DNN layer that connects every neuron in the defined layer to every neuron in the previous layer. For instance, if Layer 1 has 5 neurons and Layer 2 (dense layer) has 3 neurons, the total number of connections between Layer 1 and Layer 2 would be 15 (5×3). Since it accommodates every possible connection between the layers, it is called a "dense" layer.

Keras offers the dense layer with the following default parameters.

```
keras.layers.Dense(units, activation=None, use_bias=True,
                   kernel_initializer='glorot_uniform',
                   bias_initializer='zeros',
                   kernel_regularizer=None,
                   bias_regularizer=None,
                   activity_regularizer=None,
                   kernel_constraint=None,
                   bias_constraint=None)
```

It offers a lot of customization for any given layer. We can specify the number of units (i.e., neurons for the layer), the activation type, the type initialization for kernel and bias, and other constraints. Most often, we just use parameters like units and activation. The rest can be left to the defaults for simplicity. These additional parameters become important when we are working in specialized use cases where the importance of using specific types of constraints and initializers for a given layer is paramount.

We also need to define the input shape for the Keras layer. The input shape needs to be defined for only the first layer. Subsequent layers just need the number of neurons defined. We can use the input_dim attribute to define how many dimensions the input has. For instance, if we have a table with 10 features and 1000 samples, we need to provide the input_dim as 10 for the layer to understand the shape of input data.

Example: A network with one hidden layer and the output layer for simple binary classification.

Layer 1 has 5 neurons and expects an input with 10 features; therefore, input_dim =10. The final layer is the output, which has one neuron.

```
model = Sequential()
model.add(Dense(5,input_dim=10,activation = "sigmoid"))
model.add(Dense(1,activation = "sigmoid"))
```

Dropout Layer

The dropout layer in DL helps reduce overfitting by introducing regularization and generalization capabilities into the model. In the literal sense, the dropout layer drops out a few neurons or sets them to 0 and reduces computation in the training process. The process of arbitrarily dropping neurons works quite well in reducing overfitting. We will take up this topic in more depth and understand the rationale behind overfitting, model generalization in Chapter 5.

Keras offers a dropout layer with the following default parameters:

```
keras.layers.Dropout(rate, noise_shape=None, seed=None)
```

We add the dropout layer after a regular layer in the DL model architecture. The following codes show a sample:

```
model = Sequential()
model.add(Dense(5,input_dim=10,activation = "sigmoid"))
model.add(Dropout(rate = 0.1,seed=100))
model.add(Dense(1,activation = "sigmoid"))
```

Other Important Layers

Considering the diversity of use cases, Keras has inbuilt defined layers for most. In computer vision use cases, the input is usually an image. There are special layers to extract features from images; they are called convolutional layers. Similarly, for natural language processing and similar use cases, there is an advanced DNN called recurrent neural network (RNN). Keras has provided several different types of recurrent layers for its development.

The list is quite long, and we won't cover the other advanced layers now. However, in order to keep you updated, here are some of the other important layers in Keras that will be handy for you for advanced use cases in the future:

- Embedding layers - `https://keras.io/layers/embeddings/`

- Convolutional layers - `https://keras.io/layers/convolutional/`

- Pooling layers - `https://keras.io/layers/pooling/`

- Merge layers - `https://keras.io/layers/merge/`

- Recurrent layers - `https://keras.io/layers/recurrent/`

- Normalization layers and many more - `https://keras.io/layers/normalization/`

You can also write your own layers in Keras for a different type of use case. More details can be explored here: `https://keras.io/layers/writing-your-own-keras-layers/`

The Loss Function

The loss function is the metric that helps a network understand whether it is learning in the right direction. To frame the loss function in simple words, consider it as the test score you achieve in an examination. Say you appeared for several tests on the same subject: what metric would you use to understand your performance on each test? Obviously, the test score. Assume you scored 56, 60, 78, 90, and 96 out of 100 in five consecutive language tests. You would clearly see that the improving test scores are an indication of how well you are performing. Had the test scores been decreasing, then the verdict would be that your performance is decreasing and you would need to change your studying methods or materials to improve.

Similarly, how does a network understand whether it is improving its learning process in each iteration? It uses the loss function, which is analogous to the test score. The loss function essentially measures the loss from the target. Say you are developing a model to predict whether a student will pass or fail and the chance of passing or failing is defined by the probability. So, 1 would indicate that he will pass with 100% certainty and 0 would indicate that he will definitely fail.

The model learns from the data and predicts a score of 0.87 for the student to pass. So, the actual loss here would be 1.00 – 0.87 = 0.13. If it repeats the exercise with some parameter updates in order to improve and now achieves a loss of 0.40, it would understand that the changes it has made are not helping the network to appropriately learn. Alternatively, a new loss of 0.05 would indicate that the updates or changes from the learning are in the right direction.

Based on the type of data outcome, we have several standard loss functions defined in ML and DL. For regression use cases (i.e., where the end prediction would be a continuous number like the marks scored by a student, the number of product units sold by a shop, the number of calls received from customers in a contact center, etc.), here are some popular loss functions available:

- Mean Squared Error - Average squared difference between the actual and predicted value. The squared difference makes it easy to penalize the model more for a higher difference. So, a difference of 3 would result in a loss of 9, but difference of 9 would return a loss of 81.

  - The mathematical equivalent would be

  $$\sum_{n=1}^{k} \frac{\left(Actual - Predicted\right)^2}{k}$$

  - Keras equivalent

    ```
    keras.losses.mean_squared_error(y_actual,
    y_pred)
    ```

- Mean Absolute Error – The average absolute error between actual and predicted.

  - The mathematical equivalent would be

  $$\sum_{n=1}^{k} \left|Actual - Predicted\right|$$

  - Keras equivalent

    ```
    keras.losses.mean_absolute_error
    (y_actual, y_pred)
    ```

- Similarly, few other variants are

  - MAPE – Mean absolute percentage error

    ```
    keras.losses.mean_absolute_percentage_error
    ```

  - MSLE – Mean square logarithmic error

    ```
    keras.losses.mean_squared_logarithmic_error
    ```

For categorical outcomes, your prediction would be for a class, like whether a student will pass (1) or fail (0), whether the customer will make a purchase or not, whether the customer will default on payment or not, and so on. Some use cases may have multiple classes as an outcome, like classifying types of disease (Type A, B, or C), classifying images as cats, dogs, cars, horses, landscapes, and so on.

In such cases, the losses defined in the preceding cannot be used due to obvious reasons. We would need to quantify the outcome of the class as probability and define losses based on the probability estimates as predictions.

A few popular choices for losses for categorical outcomes in Keras are as follows:

- **Binary cross-entropy:** Defines the loss when the categorical outcomes is a binary variable, that is, with two possible outcomes: (Pass/Fail) or (Yes/No)

  - The mathematical form would be

    $$Loss = - [y * \log(p) + (1-y) * \log(1-p)]$$

  - Keras equivalent

    ```
    keras.losses.binary_crossentropy(y_
    actual, y_predicted)
    ```

- **Categorical cross-entropy:** Defines the loss when the categorical outcomes is a nonbinary, that is, >2 possible outcomes: (Yes/No/Maybe) or (Type 1/ Type 2/... Type n)

  - The mathematical form would be

    $$Loss = -\sum_{i}^{n} y_i' \log_2 y_i$$

  - Keras equivalent

    ```
    keras.losses.categorical_crossentropy
    (y_actual, y_predicted)
    ```

Optimizers

The most important part of the model training is the optimizer. Up to this point, we have addressed the process of giving feedback to the model through an algorithm called backpropagation; this is actually an optimization algorithm.

To add more context, imagine the model structure that you have defined to classify whether a student will pass or fail. The structure created by defining the sequence of layers with the number of neurons, the activation functions, and the input and output shape is initialized with random weights in the beginning. The weights that determined the influence of a neuron on the next neuron or the final output are updated during the learning process by the network.

In a nutshell, a network with randomized weights and a defined structure is the starting point for a model. The model can make a prediction at this point, but it would almost always be of no value. The network takes one training sample and uses its values as inputs to the neurons in the first layer, which then produces an output with the defined activation function. The output now becomes an input for the next layer, and so on. The output of the final layer would be the prediction for the training sample. This is where the loss function comes into the picture. The loss function helps the network understand how well or poorly the current set of weights has performed on the training sample. The next step for the model is to reduce the loss. How does it know what steps or updates it should perform on the weights to reduce the loss? The optimizer function helps it understand this step. The optimizer function is a mathematical algorithm that uses derivatives, partial derivatives, and the chain rule in calculus to understand how much change the network will see in the loss function by making a small change in the weight of the neurons. The change in the loss function, which would be an increase or decrease, helps in determining the direction of the change required in the weight of the connection. The computation of one training sample from the input layer to the output layer is called a pass. Usually, training would be done in batches due to memory constraints in the system. A batch is a collection of training samples from the entire input. The network updates its weights after processing all samples in a batch. This is called an iteration (i.e., a successful pass of all samples in a batch followed by a weight update in the network). The computing of all training samples provided in the input data with batch-by-batch weight updates is called an epoch. In each iteration, the network leverages the optimizer function to make a small change to its weight parameters (which were randomly initialized at the beginning) to improve the end prediction by reducing the loss function. Step by step, with several iterations and then several epochs, the network updates its weights and learns to make a correct prediction for the given training samples.

The mathematical explanation for the functioning of the optimizer function was abstracted in a simple way for you to understand and appreciate the background operations that happen in the DNN during the training process. The in-depth math equations and the reasoning for the optimization process are beyond the scope of this book. In case you are supercurious about learning math and the actual process of the optimization algorithm, I would recommend reading a chapter from the book *Pro Deep Learning with TensorFlow* by Santanu Pattanayak (Apress, 2017). The book does an amazing job of explaining the math behind DL with a very intuitive approach. I highly recommend this book to all PhD students exploring DL.

Given that you have a fair understanding of the overall optimization process, I would like to take a minute to discuss various optimization algorithms available in Keras.

Stochastic Gradient Descent (SGD)

SGD performs an iteration with each training sample (i.e., after the pass of every training sample, it calculates the loss and updates the weight). Since the weights are updated too frequently, the overall loss curve would be very noisy. However, the optimization is relatively fast compared to others.

The formula for weight updates can be expressed in a simple way as follows:

Weights = Weights – learning rate * Loss

Where learning rate is a parameter we define in the network architecture.

Say, for learning rate =0.01

Keras provides SGD with

```
keras.optimizers.SGD(lr=0.01, momentum=0.0, decay=0.0,
nesterov=False)
```

For updates with every training sample, we would need to use batch_ size=1 in the model training function.

To reduce high fluctuations in the SGD optimizations, a better approach would be to reduce the number of iterations by providing a minibatch, which would then enable averaging the loss for all samples in a batch and updating the weights at the end of the batch. This approach has been more successful and results in a smoother training process. Batch size is usually set in powers of 2 (i.e., 32, 64, 128, etc.).

Adam

Adam, which stands for Adaptive Moment Estimation, is by far the most popular and widely used optimizer in DL. In most cases, you can blindly choose the Adam optimizer and forget about the optimization alternatives. This optimization technique computes an adaptive learning rate for each parameter. It defines momentum and variance of the gradient of the loss and leverages a combined effect to update the weight parameters. The momentum and variance together help smooth the learning curve and effectively improve the learning process.

The math representation can be simplified in the following way:

Weights = Weights – (Momentum and Variance combined)

Keras provides the Adam optimizer as

```
keras.optimizers.Adam(lr=0.001, beta_1=0.9, beta_2=0.999,
epsilon=None, decay=0.0, amsgrad=False)
```

The parameters beta_1 and beta_2 are used in computing the momentum and variance, respectively. The default values work quite effectively and doesn't need to be changed for most use cases.

Other Important Optimizers

There are many other popular optimizers that can also be used for different DL models. Discussing all of them would be beyond the scope of this book. In the interest of keeping you well informed about the available options, I would like to list a few of the other popular optimization alternatives used and available within Keras:

- Adagrad
- Adadelta
- RMSProp
- Adamax
- Nadam

Each of the optimization techniques has its own pros and cons. A major problem which we often face in DL is the vanishing gradient and saddle point problem. You can explore these problems in more detail while choosing the best optimizer for your problem. But for most use cases, Adam always works fine.

Metrics

Similar to the loss function, we also define metrics for the model in Keras. In a simple way, metrics can be understood as the function used to judge the performance of the model on a different unseen dataset, also called the validation dataset. The only difference between metrics and the loss function is that the results from metrics are not used in training the model with respect to optimization. They are only used to validate the test results while reporting.

A few available options for metrics in Keras are as follows:

- Binary Accuracy - keras.metrics.binary_accuracy

- Categorical Accuracy - keras.metrics.caetogrical_accuracy

- Sparse Categorical Accuracy - keras.metrics.sparse_categorical_accuracy

You can also define custom functions for your model metrics. Keras provides you with the ability to easily configure a model with user-defined metrics.

Model Configuration

Now that we understand the most fundamental building blocks of a DNN in Keras, we can take a look at the final model configuration step, which orchestrates all the preceding components together.

Once you have designed your network, Keras provides you with an easy one-step model configuration process with the 'compile' command. To compile a model, we need to provide three parameters: an optimization function, a loss function, and a metric for the model to measure performance on the validation dataset.

The following example builds a DNN with two hidden layers, with 32 and 16 neurons, respectively, with a ReLU activation function. The final output is for a binary categorical numeric output using a sigmoid activation. We compile the model with the Adam optimizer and define binary cross-entropy as the loss function and "accuracy" as the metric for validation.

```
from keras.models import Sequential
from keras.layers import Dense, Activation

model = Sequential()
model.add(Dense(32, input_dim=10,activation = "relu"))
model.add(Dense(16,activation = "relu"))
model.add(Dense(1,activation = "sigmoid"))

model.compile(optimizer='Adam',loss='binary_crossentropy',
metrics=['accuracy'])
```

Model Training

Once we configure a model, we have all the required pieces for the model ready. We can now go ahead and train the model with the data. While training, it is always a good practice to provide a validation dataset for us to evaluate whether the model is performing as desired after each epoch. The model leverages the training data to train itself and learn the patterns, and at the end of each epoch, it will use the unseen validation data to make predictions and compute metrics. The performance on the validation dataset is a good cue for the overall performance.

For validation data, it is a common practice to divide your available data into three parts with a 60:20:20 ratio. We use 60% for training, 20% for validation, and the last 20% for testing. This ratio is not a mandate. You have the flexibility to change the ratio as per your choice. In general, when you have really large training datasets, say n>1MN samples, it is fine to take 95% for training, 2% for validation, and 3% for testing. Again, the ratio is a choice you make based on your judgment and available data.

Keras provides a fit function for the model object to train with the provided training data.

Here is a sample model invoking its fit method. At this point, it is assumed that you have the model architecture defined and configured (compiled) as discussed in the preceding.

```
model.fit(x_train, y_train, batch_size=64, epochs=3,
validation_data=(x_val, y_val))
```

We have a model being trained on a training dataset named x_train with the actual labels in y_train. We choose a batch size of 64. Therefore, if there were 500 training samples, the model would intake and process 64 samples at a time in a batch before it updates the model weights. The last batch may have <64 training sample if unavailable. We have set the number of epochs to three; therefore, the whole process of training 500 sample in batches of 64 will be repeated thrice. Also, we have provided the validation dataset as x_val and y_val. At the end of each epoch, the model would use the validation data to make predictions and compute the performance metrics as defined in the metrics parameter of the model configuration.

Now that we have all the pieces required for the model to be designed, configured, and trained, let's put all pieces of the puzzle together and see it in action.

```
import numpy as np
from keras.models import Sequential
from keras.layers import Dense, Activation
```

```python
# Generate dummy training dataset
np.random.seed(2018)
x_train = np.random.random((6000,10))
y_train = np.random.randint(2, size=(6000, 1))

# Generate dummy validation dataset
x_val = np.random.random((2000,10))
y_val = np.random.randint(2, size=(2000, 1))

# Generate dummy test dataset
x_test = np.random.random((2000,10))
y_test = np.random.randint(2, size=(2000, 1))

#Define the model architecture
model = Sequential()
model.add(Dense(64, input_dim=10,activation = "relu")) #Layer 1
model.add(Dense(32,activation = "relu"))                #Layer 2
model.add(Dense(16,activation = "relu"))                #Layer 3
model.add(Dense(8,activation = "relu"))                 #Layer 4
model.add(Dense(4,activation = "relu"))                 #Layer 5
model.add(Dense(1,activation = "sigmoid"))              #Output
                                                        Layer

#Configure the model
model.compile(optimizer='Adam',loss='binary_crossentropy',metri
cs=['accuracy'])

#Train the model
model.fit(x_train, y_train, batch_size=64, epochs=3,
validation_data=(x_val,y_val))
```

The output while training the model is showcased in the following:

```
Train on 6000 samples, validate on 2000 samples
Epoch 1/3
6000/6000 [==============================] - 2s 363us/step - loss: 0.6934 - acc: 0.4972 - val_loss: 0.6932 - val_acc:
0.4945
Epoch 2/3
6000/6000 [==============================] - 0s 58us/step - loss: 0.6933 - acc: 0.4993 - val_loss: 0.6934 - val_acc:
0.4945
Epoch 3/3
6000/6000 [==============================] - 0s 55us/step - loss: 0.6931 - acc: 0.5045 - val_loss: 0.6933 - val_acc:
0.5110
```

We can see that after every epoch, the model prints the mean training loss and accuracy as well as the validation loss and accuracy. We can use these intermediate results to make a judgment on the model performance. In most large DL use cases, we would have several epochs for training. It is a good practice to keep a track of the model performance with the metrics we have configured at intervals to see the results after a few epochs. If the results don't seem in your favor, it might be a good idea to stop the training and revisit the model architecture and configuration.

Model Evaluation

In all of the preceding examples, we have looked into a specific portion of the model development step or we have concluded with model training. We haven't discussed model performance so far. Understanding how effectively your model is performing on an unseen test dataset is of paramount importance.

Keras provides the model object equipped with inbuilt model evaluation and another function to predict the outcome from a test dataset. Let's have a look at both of these using the trained model and dummy test data generated in the preceding example.

The method provided by Keras for the sequential model is as shown in the following:

```
evaluate(x=None, y=None, batch_size=None, verbose=1, sample_
weight=None, steps=None)
```

We provide the test data and the test labels in the parameters x and y. In cases where the test data is also huge and expected to consume a significant amount of memory, you can use the batch size to tell the Keras model to make predictions batch-wise and then consolidate all results.

```
print(model.evaluate(x_test,y_test))
[0.6925005965232849, 0.521]
```

In the evaluate method, the model returns the loss value and all metrics defined in the model configuration. These metric labels are available in the model property metrics_names.

```
print(model.metrics_names)
['loss', 'acc']
```

We can therefore see that the model has an overall accuracy of 52% on the test dataset. This is definitely not a good model result, but it was expected given that we used just a dummy dataset.

Alternatively, you could use the predict method of the model and leverage the actual predictions that would be probabilities (for this use case, since binary classification):

```
#Make predictions on the test dataset and print the first 10
predictions
pred = model.predict(x_test)
pred[:10]
```

Output

```
array([[0.4989694 ],
       [0.5111768 ],
       [0.4981183 ],
       [0.50972915],
       [0.5059872 ],
       [0.50466985],
       [0.5042962 ],
       [0.5179587 ],
       [0.5002746 ],
       [0.5066786 ]], dtype=float32)
```

This output can be used to make even more refined final predictions. A simple example is that the model would use 0.5 as the threshold for the predictions. Therefore, any predicted value above 0.5 is classified as 1 (say, Pass), and others as 0 (Fail).

Depending on your use case, you might want to slightly tweak your prediction for more aggressive correct prediction for 1 (Pass), so you might choose a threshold at 0.6 instead of 0.5, or vice versa.

Putting All the Building Blocks Together

I hope you can now make sense of the first DNN model we saw in the last section of Chapter 1. Before understanding all the basic building blocks, it would have been overwhelming to grasp the reasoning for the code used in the model development.

Now that we have all the basic necessary ingredients ready, let's look at more tangible use case before we conclude this chapter. To do so, let's take a better dataset and see what things look like. Keras also provides a few datasets to play with. These are real datasets and are usually used by most beginners during their initial experiments with ML and DL.

For our experiment, let's select a popular Keras dataset for developing a model. We can start with the Boston House Prices dataset. It is taken from the StatLib library, which is maintained at Carnegie Mellon University. The data is present in an Amazon S2 bucket, which we can download by using simple Keras commands provided exclusively for the datasets.

```
#Download the data using Keras; this will need an active
internet connection
from keras.datasets import boston_housing
(x_train, y_train), (x_test, y_test) = boston_housing.load_
data()
```

The dataset is directly downloaded into the Python environment and is ready to use. Let's have a look at what the data looks like. We will use basic Python commands to look at the type of data, its length and breadth, and a preview of the content.

```
#Explore the data structure using basic python commands
print("Type of the Dataset:",type(y_train))
print("Shape of training data :",x_train.shape)
print("Shape of training labels :",y_train.shape)
print("Shape of testing data :",type(x_test))
print("Shape of testing labels :",y_test.shape)
```

Output

```
Type of the Dataset: <class 'numpy.ndarray'>
Shape of training data : (404, 13)
Shape of training labels : (404,)
Shape of testing data : <class 'numpy.ndarray'>
Shape of testing labels : (102,)
```

We can see that the training and test datasets are Python numpy arrays. Numpy is a Python library to handle large multidimensional arrays. We have 404 rows of data with 13 features in the training dataset and 102 rows with the same number of features in the test dataset. Overall, it's approximately an 80:20 ratio between train and test. We can further divide the 402 rows of training data into 300 for training and 102 for validation.

Alright, the data structure and its shape look great. Let's have a quick look at the contents of the dataset. The preceding code showcased that we have 13 columns in the data. To understand the actual column names, we would need to refer to the data dictionary provided by CMU. You can find more details about the dataset here: http://lib.stat.cmu.edu/datasets/boston.

The description for the features in the data is showcased in the following list. The last row in the list refers to the label or the actual house price in our use case.

Column Name	Description
CRIM	per capita crime rate by town
ZN	proportion of residential land zoned for lots over 25,000 sq. ft.
INDUS	proportion of nonretail business acres per town
CHAS	Charles River dummy variable (= 1 if tract bounds river; 0 otherwise)
NOX	nitric oxide concentration (parts per 10 million)
RM	average number of rooms per dwelling
AGE	proportion of owner-occupied units built prior to 1940
DIS	weighted distances to five Boston employment centers
RAD	index of accessibility to radial highways
TAX	full-value property tax rate per $10,000
PTRATIO	pupil-teacher ratio by town
B	$1000(Bk - 0.63)^2$, where Bk is the proportion of blacks by town
LSTAT	% lower status of the population
MEDV	median value of owner-occupied homes in $1000's

To look at the contents of the training dataset, we can use the index-slicing option provided by Python's numpy library for the numpy n-dimensional arrays.

```
x_train[:3,:]
```

Output

```
array([[1.23247e+00, 0.00000e+00, 8.14000e+00, 0.00000e+00,
        5.38000e-01, 6.14200e+00, 9.17000e+01, 3.97690e+00,
        4.00000e+00, 3.07000e+02, 2.10000e+01, 3.96900e+02,
        1.87200e+01],
       [2.17700e-02, 8.25000e+01, 2.03000e+00, 0.00000e+00,
        4.15000e-01, 7.61000e+00, 1.57000e+01, 6.27000e+00,
        2.00000e+00, 3.48000e+02, 1.47000e+01, 3.95380e+02,
        3.11000e+00],
       [4.89822e+00, 0.00000e+00, 1.81000e+01, 0.00000e+00,
        6.31000e-01, 4.97000e+00, 1.00000e+02, 1.33250e+00,
        2.40000e+01, 6.66000e+02, 2.02000e+01, 3.75520e+02,
        3.26000e+00]])
```

All columns have numeric values, so there is no need for data transformation. Usually, once we have imported the dataset, we will need to extensively explore the data and will almost always clean, process, and augment it before we can start developing the models.

But for now, we will directly go ahead with a simple model and see what the results look like.

```
import numpy as np
from keras.models import Sequential
from keras.layers import Dense, Activation

#Extract the last 100 rows from the training data to create the
validation datasets.
x_val = x_train[300:,]
y_val = y_train[300:,]
```

```
#Define the model architecture
model = Sequential()
model.add(Dense(13, input_dim=13, kernel_initializer='normal',
activation='relu'))
model.add(Dense(6, kernel_initializer='normal',
activation='relu'))
model.add(Dense(1, kernel_initializer='normal'))

# Compile model
model.compile(loss='mean_squared_error', optimizer='adam',
metrics=['mean_absolute_percentage_error'])

#Train the model
model.fit(x_train, y_train, batch_size=32, epochs=3,
validation_data=(x_val,y_val))
```

Output

```
Train on 404 samples, validate on 104 samples
Epoch 1/3
404/404 [==============================] - 2s 4ms/step - loss:
598.8595 - mean_absolute_percentage_error: 101.7889 - val_loss:
681.4912 - val_mean_absolute_percentage_error: 100.0789
Epoch 2/3
404/404 [==============================] - 0s 81us/step - loss:
583.6991 - mean_absolute_percentage_error: 99.7594 - val_loss:
674.8345 - val_mean_absolute_percentage_error: 99.2616
Epoch 3/3
404/404 [==============================] - 0s 94us/step - loss:
573.6101 - mean_absolute_percentage_error: 98.3180 - val_loss:
654.3787 - val_mean_absolute_percentage_error: 96.9662
```

We have created a simple two-hidden-layer model for the regression use case. We have chosen MAPE as the metric. Generally, this is not the best metric to choose for studying model performance, but its advantage is simplicity in terms of comprehending the results. It gives a simple percentage value for the error, say 10% error. So, if you know the average range of your prediction, you can easily estimate what the predictions are going to look like.

Let's now train the model and use the evaluate function to study the results of the model.

```
results = model.evaluate(x_test, y_test)

for i in range(len(model.metrics_names)):
    print(model.metrics_names[i]," : ", results[i])
```

Output

```
102/102 [==============================] - 0s 87us/step
loss  :   589.7658882889093
mean_absolute_percentage_error  :   96.48218611174939
```

We can see that MAPE is around 96%, which is actually not a great number to have for model performance. This would translate into our model predictions at around 96% error. So, in general, if a house was priced at 10K, our model would have predicted ~20K.

In DL, the model updates weight after every iteration and evaluates after every epoch. Since the updates are quite small, it usually takes a fairly higher number of epochs for a generic model to learn appropriately. To test the performance once again, let's increase the number of epochs to 30 instead of 3. This would increase the computation significantly and might take a while to execute. But since this is a fairly small dataset, training with 30 epochs should not be a problem. It should execute in ~1 min on your system.

```
#Train the model
model.fit(x_train, y_train, batch_size=32, epochs=30,
validation_data=(x_val,y_val))
```

Output

```
Train on 404 samples, validate on 104 samples
Epoch 1/1000
404/404 [==============================] - 0s 114us/step -
loss: 536.6662 - mean_absolute_percentage_error: 93.4381 - val_
loss: 580.3155 - val_mean_absolute_percentage_error: 88.6968
Epoch 2/1000
404/404 [==============================] - 0s 143us/step -
loss: 431.7025 - mean_absolute_percentage_error: 79.0697 - val_
loss: 413.4064 - val_mean_absolute_percentage_error: 67.0769
```

Skipping the output for in-between epochs.

(Adding output for only the last three epochs, i.e., 28 to 30)

```
Epoch 28/30
404/404 [==============================] - 0s 111us/step -
loss: 6.0758 - mean_absolute_percentage_error: 9.5185 - val_
loss: 5.2524 - val_mean_absolute_percentage_error: 8.3853
Epoch 29/30
404/404 [==============================] - 0s 100us/step -
loss: 6.2895 - mean_absolute_percentage_error: 10.1037 - val_
loss: 6.0818 - val_mean_absolute_percentage_error: 8.9386
Epoch 30/30
404/404 [==============================] - 0s 111us/step -
loss: 6.0761 - mean_absolute_percentage_error: 9.8201 - val_   .
loss: 7.3844 - val_mean_absolute_percentage_error: 8.9812
```

If we take a closer look at the loss and MAPE for the validation datasets, we can see a significant improvement. It has reduced from 96% in the previous example to 8.9% now.

Let's have a look at the test results.

```
results = model.evaluate(x_test, y_test)

for i in range(len(model.metrics_names)):
    print(model.metrics_names[i]," : ", results[i])
```

Output

```
102/102 [==============================] - 0s 92us/step
loss  :  22.09559840782016
mean_absolute_percentage_error  :  16.22196163850672
```

We can see that the results have improved significantly, but there still seems to be a significant gap between the MAPE for validation dataset and the test dataset. As discussed earlier, this gap is an indicator that the model has overfit, or in simple terms, has overcomplicated the process of learning. We will look in detail at the steps to reduce overfitting in DNNs in the next chapter for a bigger and better use case. For now, we have successfully explored Keras on a real dataset (though a small one) and used our learnings on the building blocks of DL in Keras.

Summary

In this chapter, we explored Keras in depth with hands-on exercises as well as contextual depth of topics. We studied the basic building blocks of DL and its implementation in Keras. We looked at how we can combine the different building blocks together in using Keras to develop DNN models. In the next chapter, we will start exploring a real use case step by step by exploring, cleaning, extracting, and applying the necessary transformations to get the data ready for developing DL models.

CHAPTER 3

Deep Neural Networks for Supervised Learning: Regression

In Chapters 1 and 2, we explored the topic of DL and studied how DL evolved from ML to solve an interesting area of problems. We discussed the need for DL frameworks and briefly explored a few popular frameworks available in the market. We then studied why Keras is special and spent some time playing around with its basic building blocks provided to develop DNNs and also understood the intuition behind a DL model holistically. We then put together all our learnings from the practical exercises to develop a baby neural network for the Boston house prices use case.

Now that we have a fair understanding of the different DL building blocks and the associated science, let's explore a practical DNN for a regression use case in this chapter.

Getting Started

The evolution of AI as a field and the increasing number of researchers and practitioners in the field have created a mature and benevolent community. Today, it's fairly easy to access tools, research papers, datasets, and in fact even infrastructure to practice DL as a field. For our first use

© Jojo Moolayil 2019
J. Moolayil, *Learn Keras for Deep Neural Networks*,
https://doi.org/10.1007/978-1-4842-4240-7_3

case, we would need a dataset and a business problem to get started. Here are a few popular choices.

- **Kaggle:** www.kaggle.com/

  Kaggle is the world's largest community of data scientists and machine learners. It started off as an online ML competition forum and later evolved into a mature platform that is highly recommended for every individual in data science. It still hosts ML competitions and also provides ML datasets, kernels or community-developed scripts for solving ML problems, ML jobs, and a platform to develop and execute ML models for the hosted competitions and public datasets.

- **US Government Open Data:** www.data.gov/

  Provides access to thousands of datasets on agriculture, climate, finance, and so on.

- **Indian Government Open Data:** https://data.gov.in/

  Provides open datasets for India's demography, education, economy, industries, and so on.

- **Amazon Web Service Datasets:** https://registry.opendata.aws/

  Provides a few large datasets from NASA NEX and Openstreetmap, the Deutsche Bank public dataset, and so on.

- **Google Dataset Search:** https://toolbox.google.com/datasetsearch

This is relatively new and still in beta (at the writing of this book), but very promising. It provides access to thousands of public datasets for research experiments with a simple search query. It aggregates datasets from several public dataset repositories.

- **UCI ML Repository:** https://archive.ics.uci.edu/ml/

  Another popular repository to explore datasets for ML and DL.

We will use the Kaggle public data repository for getting datasets for our DL use case. We will use the Rossmann Store sales dataset, which is available at www.kaggle.com/c/rossmann-store-sales/data. This was a very popular competition hosted a couple of years ago and has a fairly large dataset. You would need to register with Kaggle and accept the competition rules to be able to download the data. In case you have not already registered with Kaggle, I would highly recommend doing it. Every data science professional should keep a close watch on Kaggle for its great learning, experimentation, and discussion platform for data science.

From the datasets, you need only train.csv and store.csv, which are around 38MB and 45KB, respectively. Please download the data and keep it ready in a separate folder.

Problem Statement

Rossmann is one of the largest drugstore chains in Germany, with operations across Europe. As of 2018, they have well over 3,900 stores in Europe with an annual turnover of 9 billion euros. Our task is to predict the sales for a few identified stores on a given day.

Now, let's look at the problem from a pure business perspective. The first question you would need to ask is: who is the end stakeholder for the business problem and how is he going to utilize the solution? Well, given that this was an online data science competition, we won't have a validated answer for this question, but we can more or less figure out what one would look like.

First, we need to reframe the problem statement in a slightly strategic way to be able to represent the problem statement as a design solution. There are several problem-solving frameworks recognized by the market to help define and represent a problem statement in a standard way to be more effective in solving the problem. McKinsey's "Situation–Complication–Resolution" (SCR) and Mu Sigma Inc.'s "Situation Complication Question" (SCQ) are among the most popular frameworks. We will leverage one of the aforementioned frameworks to represent our problem statement in a more effective and concise way. But let us first understand why this would be important.

Why Is Representing a Problem Statement with a Design Principle Important?

Most large, complex problems need detailed design, peer reviews, validation of approach and strategy, a ton of brainstorming, and probably even a small proof of concept before getting started. Enterprise software development is a classic example. You would have a team defining the business requirements and documenting them for future reference, designing a high-level diagram followed by a low-level design and eventually detailing the specifics for each software component and how the end solution would look. At any point in time, if a new engineer joins the team to collaborate, the design documents, approach, and business requirements would help him understand the larger picture without the need for individual discussions. Also, at any point in time the design and approach help in the smooth execution of the overall objective.

Problems in data science and ML/DL need a similar approach before any work is started. While it may not be possible for the entire solution to be drafted at the beginning, given that the entire process is iterative and exploratory, we could still do a better job of representing the problem and a high-level approach to the solution. To understand a problem definition framed with design principles, let's have a look at one.

Designing an SCQ

The SCQ framework designed and published by Mu Sigma Inc. is a popular framework used to represent a problem in consulting companies. It divides the problem into three simple groups, expands each group with the right question, and finally connects with the desired future state.

The four components can be defined as follows:

- **Desired Future State**

    The end state we want to reach when the problem is solved.

- **Situation**

    A brief narrative of the overall problem statement that details the problem faced by the stakeholder. This is usually wrapped in two lines at most.

- **Complication**

    Defines the major roadblock that hinders the stakeholder's transition from the current situation to the desired future situation.

- **Question**

    The key question that needs to be answered in order to mitigate the roadblock.

For our use case, we can define the SCQ as showcased in the following illustration.

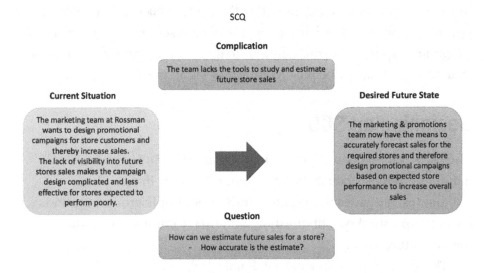

With the SCQ, we now have a more holistic understanding of the problem statement. We know that there is a marketing team designing store-specific promotional campaigns to target customers and increase the overall revenue while using resources more judiciously. Therefore, they don't want to provide promotions to stores that would be outperforming anyway irrespective of the promotions. If they have visibility into estimated future sales, they can classify a few stores as "low," "medium," and "high" based on a defined threshold for the required discount and promotions to achieve the expected targets.

The team hit a roadblock, as they have no means to estimate the future sales for a given store. Therefore, to solve the problem, we ask the following question: "How can we estimate future sales for a store?" Given that the roadblock has been overcome, the marketing team now has the means to study and estimate future store sales and thus design more effective promotional campaigns.

Designing the Solution

The answer to the key question of the business problem is probably easy to guess now. We are going to develop an ML model that can learn the sales for a store as a function of internal, external, and temporal (time-based) attributes and then predict future sales given the attributes available.

This might seem like a time-series forecasting problem, a scenario where we purely define sales or a similar target as a function of time (i.e., considering historic weekly or daily sales and projecting the future data points by simulating the trend and patterns). But this is feasible only for scenarios where we have to make estimates for just 1 store. For 1000 stores, manually studying weekly sales and developing models to estimate future sales is a laborious and mostly nonviable solution. Alternatively, we can approach this problem using a global time-series model (i.e., just develop one single model that will be used for all stores). While this is definitely possible, the results of the forecast will add no value to the stakeholder, as it will most likely be way off the mark.

We could instead develop a more effective model by transforming this problem from a time-series forecasting problem into a regression problem. In case this is difficult to comprehend, let's make it simple using an example. The data available for any use case can be classified as time-series or cross-sectional. In time-series data, every training sample (i.e., one row of data) has a relationship with another sample associated with the time sequence. Daily or weekly sales are an appropriate example for time-series data, as one week's sales have a relationship with those of the previous weeks. In cross-sectional data, each training sample is independent and has no time-based relationship with other samples. Ad clicks by customers or transactions made by credit customers through a credit card provider are examples of cross-sectional data. There isn't a time-based relation between the two samples.

In our use case, we can consider the data in way that it can be represented as

sales as a function of store + other attributes

Instead of a time-series based model defined as

Sales as a function of time

In this way, we can define a model that can learn the patterns from various stores and other external attributes (which we will explore with the data) to predict the expected sales. The process will be clear as we explore the data and get closer to model development. Let us now get started by exploring the data.

Exploring the Data

I hope you have already downloaded the dataset from the Kaggle link after registering an account and accepting the competition rules. In case you have not, here are the steps in detail:

1. Go to Kaggle's homepage: `www.kaggle.com`

2. Create a new account using "Signup" or sign in using an existing account.

   Go to Rossmann Store Sales Competition: `www.kaggle.com/c/rossmann-store-sales/data`

3. Navigate to the middle of the page to find the "Download All" option. You will get a Competition Rules page, which you will have to read and then accept the conditions. Once they are accepted, the download will be available.

4. Unzip and move the downloaded datasets to a new folder for the exercise.

There are two important files that you need:

- train.csv

- store.csv

Once the data is ready, we can get started with Python to explore and analyze the data. You can open Jupyter Notebooks, which is already installed with Anaconda as discussed in Chapter 2. Please use the command 'jupyter notebook' in your terminal or command prompt and press Enter; then, Jupyter should open in your default browser. You can create a new notebook for our DL exercise. Alternatively, you can also use any Python IDE or Spyder IDE from Anaconda; however, Jupyter is highly recommended.

To explore data, we need basic Python commands. We will use the lazy programming approach to learn data exploration with Python; that is, we will discuss the nuances of a code block or a new package as and when we encounter it. In case you are new to Python, just reading through the code blocks along with the comments and then going through the explanation for the code block should suffice.

Let us first import the data into our system to start analyzing. The following code snippet imports the Python package 'pandas', which provides readily available functions to import, explore, manipulate, transform, visualize, and also export data in the required forms.

```
import pandas as pd
df = pd.read_csv("/Users/jojomoolayil/Book/Ch3/Data/train.csv")
```

The data is imported into the variable df. Since Python is object oriented, we can now use the pandas-associated functions as the method of the object.

Once we have the data imported, the first thing we need to explore is the length, breadth, and type of data. The following snippet prints the shape of the data as length × breadth and then showcases the first five rows of the dataset.

```
print("Shape of the Dataset:",df.shape)
#the head method displays the first 5 rows of the data
df.head(5)
```

Output

Shape of the Dataset: (1017209, 9)

	Store	DayOfWeek	Date	Sales	Customers	Open	Promo	StateHoliday	SchoolHoliday
0	1	5	2015-07-31	5263	555	1	1	0	1
1	2	5	2015-07-31	6064	625	1	1	0	1
2	3	5	2015-07-31	8314	821	1	1	0	1
3	4	5	2015-07-31	13995	1498	1	1	0	1
4	5	5	2015-07-31	4822	559	1	1	0	1

Similarly, let us import the second dataset, store.csv, and have a look at its length, breadth, and the first 5 rows.

```
store = pd.read_csv("/Users/jojomoolayil/Book/Ch3/Data/store.csv")
print("Shape of the Dataset:",store.shape)
```

```
#Display the first 5 rows of data using the head method of
pandas dataframe
store.head(5)
```

Output

Shape of the Dataset: (1115, 10)

Store	StoreType	Assortment	CompetitionDistance	CompetitionOpenSinceMonth	CompetitionOpenSinceYear	Promo2	Promo2SinceWeek	Promo2SinceYear	PromoInterval
1	c	a	1270.0	9.0	2008.0	0	NaN	NaN	NaN
2	a	a	570.0	11.0	2007.0	1	13.0	2010.0	Jan,Apr,Jul,Oct
3	a	a	14130.0	12.0	2006.0	1	14.0	2011.0	Jan,Apr,Jul,Oct
4	c	c	620.0	9.0	2009.0	0	NaN	NaN	NaN
5	a	a	29910.0	4.0	2015.0	0	NaN	NaN	NaN

As you can see, the train dataset has 1,017,209 rows and 9 columns. The head method showcases the first 5 rows of the dataframe, and we can have a look at the contents in the data by glancing through the self-explanatory column names. In the train dataset, we have data for stores on different days. We have the total sales for the particular day and a couple of additional attributes.

Likewise, the store data has 1,115 rows and 10 columns of data. It gives us additional store attributes that describe store features like assortment type, presence of competition, and promotion-related attributes.

Looking at the Data Dictionary

Let us have a look at the data dictionary provided in the competition page on Kaggle. In case you missed it, you can read through some definitions here.

- **Store:** a unique ID for each store

- **Sales:** the turnover for a given day (our target y variable)

- **Customers:** the number of customers on a given day

- **Open:** an indicator for whether the store was open: 0 = closed, 1 = open

- **StateHoliday:** indicates a state holiday. Normally all stores, with few exceptions, are closed on state holidays. Note that all schools are closed on public holidays and weekends. a = public holiday, b = Easter holiday, c = Christmas, 0 = none

- **SchoolHoliday:** indicates if the (Store, Date) was affected by the closure of public schools

- **StoreType:** differentiates between four different store models: a, b, c, d

- **Assortment:** describes an assortment level: a = basic, b = extra, c = extended

- **CompetitionDistance:** distance in meters to the nearest competitor store

- **CompetitionOpenSince[Month/Year]:** gives the approximate year and month of the time the nearest competitor was opened

- **Promo:** indicates whether a store is running a promo on that day

- **Promo2:** Promo2 is a continuing and consecutive promotion for some stores: 0 = store is not participating, 1 = store is participating

- **Promo2Since[Year/Week]:** describes the year and calendar week when the store started participating in Promo2

- **PromoInterval:** describes the consecutive intervals at which Promo2 is started, naming the months the promotion is started anew (e.g., "Feb, May, Aug, Nov" means each round starts in February, May, August, and November of any given year for that store)

To have all the data points together, we need to create one single dataframe with the store and promotion features. We can achieve this by joining the two dataframes on the 'store' column, which represents the store ID. Pandas provides a 'merge' function that is analogous to the join statement in SQL. We can perform left, right, inner, and full outer joins on one or more dataframes using one or more columns as the joining key.

The following code snippet joins the train and store dataframe to create a new dataframe.

```
df_new = df.merge(store,on=["Store"], how="inner")
print(df_new.shape)
```

Output

```
(1017209, 18)
```

The shape shows us that we have all the columns from the two dataframes in one unified dataframe. A simple check on the number of rows, which in our case is consistent, helps us understand that the join worked in the expected way.

Now that we have the data in a unified form, let us start exploring the dataset to understand a few important questions like the following: How many stores do we have the data for? How long do we have the data for? What do the average sales for a day look like? are the stores very different from each other in daily sales? Let's find out.

We will start by finding the number of unique stores in the data, the number of unique days for which we have data, and the average sales for all stores.

```
print("Distinct number of Stores :", len(df_new["Store"].
unique()))
print("Distinct number of Days :", len(df_new["Date"].
unique()))
print("Average daily sales of all stores : ",round(df_new
["Sales"].mean(),2))
```

Output

```
Distinct number of Stores : 1115
Distinct number of Days : 942
Average daily sales of all stores :  5773.82
```

We can see that there are in total 1,115 unique stores with data for 942 unique days, with an average daily sale of 5,773.

The unique method of the pandas dataframe returns the list of unique elements for the selected column, and the len function returns the total number of elements in the list. The mean method of the dataframe returns the average for the selected column, in our case the sales.

As you probably have noticed, playing around with Python is extremely simple. For almost every mainstream task that can be performed on data, pandas provides a simple method that can be leveraged with a few parameters. Let's continue exploring the dataset to understand the other columns.

Finding Data Types

We need to know what kind of data type each element in the dataframe has. So far, we have only seen the actual content in the dataset; a column which appears numerical might internally be stored as a character. Let's take a look at the data type of each column in the final merged dataset.

```
df_new.dtypes
```

Output

```
Store              int64
DayOfWeek          int64
Date               object
Sales              int64
Customers          int64
Open               int64
Promo              int64
StateHoliday       object
SchoolHoliday      int64
StoreType          object
```

```
Assortment                      object
CompetitionDistance            float64
CompetitionOpenSinceMonth      float64
CompetitionOpenSinceYear       float64
Promo2                           int64
Promo2SinceWeek                float64
Promo2SinceYear                float64
PromoInterval                   object
dtype: object
```

We see a mix of data types here, mostly int and the rest as object or float. Object in Python is a form of the character data type. Technically, we have to understand each and very column or feature in the dataset to be able to develop effective models. In model development, the majority of the time is consumed in data engineering, cleansing, and exploring.

Working with Time

We now have a fair understanding of the Store column; let's have a look at the DayOfWeek feature.

```
df_new["DayOfWeek"].value_counts()
```

Output

```
5    145845
4    145845
3    145665
2    145664
7    144730
6    144730
1    144730
Name: DayOfWeek, dtype: int64
```

As we would expect, we can see seven distinct values, with similar numbers of records in each, for the "day of the week" feature. Given that we already have the date as a feature, we could have directly used the date column to create the day of the week and also create a few other features. Let's create additional features that will help our model learn patterns better. We will create the week number, month, day, quarter, and year as features from the date variable. Similarly, since we are already creating time-related features, we can add a new feature based on climate and seasons. Considering that the stores are in Europe, we can refer to the standard season cycles and create a new season feature with values of Spring, Summer, Fall, and Winter. Pandas provides easy-to-use functions to extract date-related features; the season-related feature can be created with a simple 'if else' equivalent convention.

```
#We can extract all date properties from a datetime datatype
import numpy as np
df_new['Date'] = pd.to_datetime(df_new['Date'], infer_datetime_
format=True)
df_new["Month"] = df_new["Date"].dt.month
df_new["Quarter"] = df_new["Date"].dt.quarter
df_new["Year"] = df_new["Date"].dt.year
df_new["Day"] = df_new["Date"].dt.day
df_new["Week"] = df_new["Date"].dt.week

df_new["Season"] = np.where(df_new["Month"].isin([3,4,5]),"Spring",
                   np.where(df_new["Month"].isin([6,7,8]),
                   "Summer",
                       np.where(df_new["Month"].isin
                       ([9,10,11]),"Fall",
                           np.where(df_new["Month"].isin
                           ([12,1,2]),"Winter","None"))))
```

```
#Using the head command to view (only) the data and the newly
engineered features
print(df_new[["Date","Year","Month","Day","Week","Quarter",
"Season"]].head())
```

Output

	Date	Year	Month	Day	Week	Quarter	Season
0	2015-07-31	2015	7	31	31	3	Summer
1	2015-07-30	2015	7	30	31	3	Summer
2	2015-07-29	2015	7	29	31	3	Summer
3	2015-07-28	2015	7	28	31	3	Summer
4	2015-07-27	2015	7	27	31	3	Summer

Predicting Sales

The next feature in the list is the Sales column. This is our target variable
(i.e., we are developing the model to predict the variable).

```
#Import matplotlib, python most popular data visualizing
library
import matplotlib.pyplot as plt
%matplotlib inline

#Create a histogram to study the Daily Sales for the stores
plt.figure(figsize=(15,8))
plt.hist(df_new["Sales"])
plt.title("Histogram for Store Sales")
plt.xlabel("bins")
plt.xlabel("Frequency")
plt.show()
```

Output

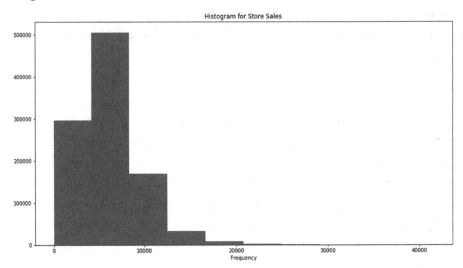

The histogram helps us understand the distribution of the data at a high level. From the preceding plot, we can see that the data range is from 0 to 40,000, but there is barely any data after 20,000. This indicates that most of the stores have sales in the range 0–20,000, and just a few stores have sales greater than 20,000. It might be worthwhile to remove these outliers, as it helps the model learn better.

Exploring Numeric Columns

Moving on, we have few more numeric columns to explore. To save time, we can use the hist function provided within pandas. Pandas also provides a plotting functionality by internally encompassing matplotlib. The following command helps us visualize a histogram for all numeric columns within the dataset.

```
#Use the  histogram function provided by the Pandas object
#The function returns a cross-tab histogram plot for all
numeric columns in the data
df_new.hist(figsize=(20,10))
```

Output

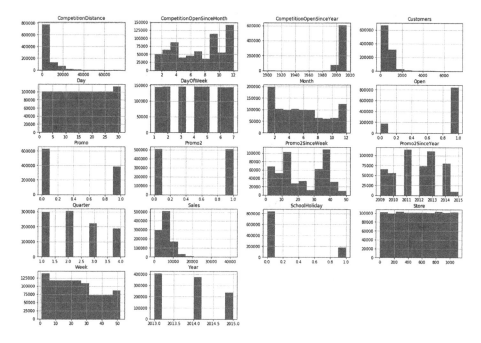

Let's analyze the results from the histogram showcased in the preceding illustration. We can see that the features Promo, Promo2, School Holiday, and Open are actually binary categorical features: they represent two possible values similar to gender: Male or Female. Therefore, these are actually categorical features but already encoded as numeric columns. This is great; we won't need to further process them, as DL models understand only numeric values.

Promo2 is well distributed between the two distinct values, whereas Promo has more records for '1' and Open has most of the store records as '1.' The distribution between the values for 'Open' makes sense, as the stores will be open for most days except state holidays.

Customer numbers range from 0 to 2,000 for most stores. A few stores have as many as 7000 daily customers, but these are outliers and we might need to fix them before modeling.

The next set of numeric variables are Promo2SinceWeek and Promo2SinceYear; these show a relatively well-distributed feature. The rest of the histograms are pretty much self-explanatory.

We have missed checking on one important aspect: is there any missing data in the dataset? The preceding plots usually don't account for missing values; instead, they exclude the null values in the plot.

Let's have a look at the number of missing data points in each column (if any) in its associated percentage form.

The isnull() command for the dataframe returns a matrix with the truth value for all data points, whether it is null or not. Passing this output into the sum function counts the number of nulls within each group. We have further divided this number by the total number of rows and multiplied it by 100 to get the final number in percentage form.

```
df_new.isnull().sum()/df_new.shape[0] * 100
```

Output

Store	0.000000
DayOfWeek	0.000000
Date	0.000000
Sales	0.000000
Customers	0.000000
Open	0.000000
Promo	0.000000
StateHoliday	0.000000
SchoolHoliday	0.000000
StoreType	0.000000
Assortment	0.000000
CompetitionDistance	0.259730
CompetitionOpenSinceMonth	31.787764
CompetitionOpenSinceYear	31.787764
Promo2	0.000000

```
Promo2SinceWeek                49.943620
Promo2SinceYear                49.943620
PromoInterval                  49.943620
Month                           0.000000
Quarter                         0.000000
Year                            0.000000
Day                             0.000000
Week                            0.000000
dtype: float64
```

The highlighted rows showcase the high number of missing data
points in the respective columns. We can see that Promo2SinceWeek,
Promo2SinceYear, PromoInterval, CompetitionOpenSinceMonth, and
CompetitionOpenSinceYear have over 30% null values. This is a big
loss and there is nothing much we can do to fix this. As a rule of thumb,
if there is a loss of anything between 0% and 10%, we can make a few
attempts to fill the missing points and use the feature. But, 30% technically
becomes beyond the usable range. On the other hand, we can see
CompetitionDistance has around 0.25% missing values. This would much
easier to handle and fix.

There are several ways we can treat missing data points. The most
common methods, like replace with mean and replace with mode, are easy
to use and work relatively well. However, this would completely depend on
your feature. If there is a 2% loss in a very crucial feature, you might want to
leverage a better estimation approach to fill in the gaps. Popular techniques
in such scenarios are clustering for missing value treatment, developing
smaller regression models for estimating the missing values, *and so on.*

For now, in this use case, we will use the mode to fill in the gaps where
we have missing values. This is as simple as finding the mode (the most
frequent value in the columns) for the column, ignoring the nulls and
replacing all nulls with the mode. The following code snippet showcases
the approach in Python.

73

```
#Replace nulls with the mode
df_new["CompetitionDistance"]=df_new["CompetitionDistance"].
fillna(df_new["CompetitionDistance"].mode()[0])
```

```
#Double check if we still see nulls for the column
df_new["CompetitionDistance"].isnull().sum()/df_new.shape[0] * 100
```

Output

```
0.0
```

Understanding the Categorical Features

Now that we have a basic understanding of all numeric features, let us now have a look at the categorical features. All in all, we have StoreType, Assortment, and the newly created Season feature as the categorical features. Though 'Open', 'Promo', 'Promo2', *and so on* are binary categorical variables, they have been stored as numeric values and already have been showcased in the histogram for our study. Let's now spend some time with the remaining three features. The best way to study a categorical variable is to study the impact on the target variable from its individual classes. We can do this by plotting the mean sales across different values of the classes in the feature. To accomplish this, we can leverage "seaborn," another powerful and easy-to-use Python visualization library, similar to matplotlib but providing much more beautiful visuals.

```
import seaborn as sns  #Seaborn is another powerful
visualization library for Python
sns.set(style="whitegrid")
```

```
#Create the bar plot for Average Sales across different Seasons
ax = sns.barplot(x="Season", y="Sales", data=df_new)
```

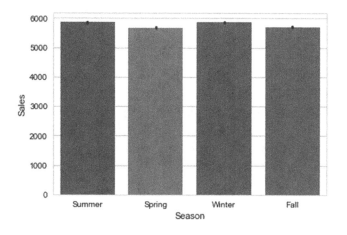

```
#Create the bar plot for Average Sales across different
Assortments
ax = sns.barplot(x="Assortment", y="Sales", data=df_new)
```

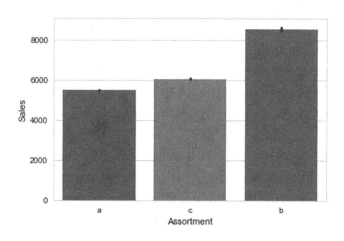

```
#Create the bar plot for Average Sales across different Store
Types
ax = sns.barplot(x="StoreType", y="Sales", data=df_new)
```

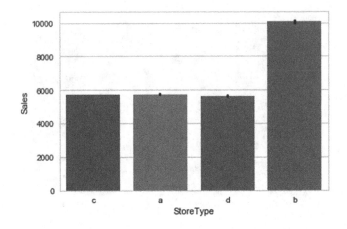

As you can see, the seaborn package has internally calculated the average sales across its classes for the provided categorical column and displayed a beautiful bar plot showcasing the relationship with our target variable. We can change the aggregation function to a different one if required; this can be changed by using the 'estimator' parameter within the `barplot` function. Sales across seasons barely seem to differ; however, there seems to be an increasing trend for sales across assortments. Stores with assortment "b" generally have the highest sales. Store type also shows a unique relationship with sales across store types. We can see fairly higher sales for "b" store types also. However, before we conclude our observations, there is one more sanity check required to validate these hypotheses. What if the number of stores in the different types mentioned in the preceding is disproportionate or skewed? In such a scenario, our observation might be flawed. To cement our understanding about the observation, we can simply check the number of data points across each category using the same `barplot` function with one additional parameter setting. We will use a new aggregation function to showcase the counts as the metric for bar charts. The following code snippet visualizes the bar plots for the same set of categorical variables we studied earlier, albeit for counts.

```
ax = sns.barplot(x="Season", y="Sales", data=df_new,
estimator=np.size)
```

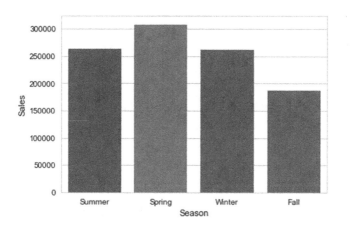

```
ax = sns.barplot(x="Assortment", y="Sales", data=df_new,
estimator=np.size)
```

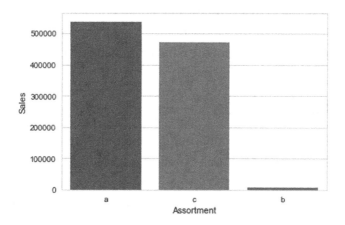

```
ax = sns.barplot(x="StoreType", y="Sales", data=df_new,
estimator=np.size)
```

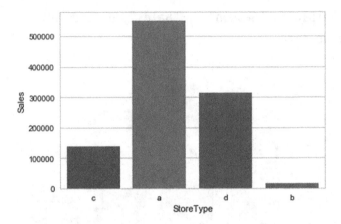

We can notice that the distribution of data points across different classes within a category is skewed. A simple check on StoreType and Assortment reveals that b has a significantly lower number of stores or data points in the dataset. Therefore, our initial understanding of the relationships observed is not true.

So, given that we have explored the length, breadth, content, nature, and summary of the dataset and further studied the continuous (numeric) as well as categorical features individually to get a good sense of the data, we can now proceed to prepare the data for developing DL models.

Data Engineering

As already mentioned, DL models understand only numeric data. Therefore, all categorical features stored as text columns need to be converted to a one-hot encoded form for the model training data.

One-hot encoding is a simple process of representing a categorical column as an expanded binary labeled matrix. So, a categorical feature with three distinct values, say "Class A," "Class B," and "Class C," can be represented with three columns instead of one, where each column would represent a binary flag for an individual category value. This is further summarized in the following example.

One Hot Encoding

Category
Class A
Class A
Class B
Class C
Class A
Class C

Class A	Class B	Class C
1	0	0
1	0	0
0	1	0
0	0	1
1	0	0
0	0	1

In our dataset, we have three categorical variables that need transformation; they are Season, Store Type, and Assortment. However, in the context of categorical variables, the day of the week, month, day, quarter, and in fact the store ID can also be defined as categorical. This may seem counterintuitive at first go, but in reality, these features have a definite number of distinct classes; for example, the day of the week can be a value only between 1 and 7. Representing them as just a column with a number might be a bad idea in cases where there are significant differences expected on different classes. For example, sales on Sunday and Monday are completely different, but internally if Sunday = 0 and Monday = 1, Tuesday = 2 and so on, a step increase from Sunday to Monday is not the same as a step increase from Monday to Tuesday. In that context, it is a good practice to represent a categorical column in its one-hot encoded version. But where do we stop? There are cases where there are a finite but very large number of classes for a feature, say 1,000 as for the store number in our example. Will it be useful to represent store number as 1,000 features or just as 1 feature with numeric values?

The answer to this is not straightforward. The best case would definitely be to represent the store number in its one-hot encoded version, but that brings in a huge problem with the size of the data. After expanding all necessary columns, we might have a training dataset with ~1,200 wide columns and 1 million rows. This would be a dataset of 10GB. Developing a model with training data of this size might be a challenge in a normal machine with limited RAM.

To overcome this dilemma, you can revert to a simple rule of thumb: if you have good hardware resources (GPU, RAM, and computing power), go ahead with one-hot encoded transformation. But if your resources are limited, transform only those that seem most important and have a fairly small number of distinct classes. Then later, iteratively validate if the experiment was effective with model performance results. If there is a serious trade-off, you might need to reconsider the training data augmentation and the hardware infrastructure to use.

In this use case, we will start with treating Season, Assortment, Month, Year, Quarter, DayOfWeek, and StoreType in one-hot encoded form and keep aside Day, Week, and Store as continuous for the time being. We will revisit this after we build a few models and study their performance.

To transform a categorical column into a one-hot encoded version, Python provides the preprocessing module in the sklearn package with rich and easy-to-use functions. The following code snippet engineers the training dataframe into the final required form for model development.

```
#Define a variable for each type of feature
from sklearn.preprocessing import LabelEncoder
from sklearn.preprocessing import OneHotEncoder
target = ["Sales"]
numeric_columns = ["Customers","Open","Promo","Promo2",
"StateHoliday","SchoolHoliday","CompetitionDistance"]
categorical_columns = ["DayOfWeek","Quarter","Month","Year",
"StoreType","Assortment","Season"]

#Define a function that will intake the raw dataframe and the
column name and return a one hot encoded DF
def create_ohe(df, col):
    le = LabelEncoder()
    a=le.fit_transform(df_new[col]).reshape(-1,1)
    ohe = OneHotEncoder(sparse=False)
    column_names = [col+ "_"+ str(i) for i in le.classes_]
```

```
return(pd.DataFrame(ohe.fit_transform(a),columns =column_names))
```

```
#Since the above function converts the column, one at a time
#We create a loop to create the final dataset with all features
temp = df_new[numeric_columns]
for column in categorical_columns:
    temp_df = create_ohe(df_new,column)
    temp = pd.concat([temp,temp_df],axis=1)
```

The output of the preceding data engineering step can be double-checked with the shape command and the distinct data types within the dataset. If there is any noninteger column, we will be left with a final step of converting it into numeric before moving ahead.

```
print("Shape of Data:",temp.shape)
print("Distinct Datatypes:",temp.dtypes.unique())
```

Output

```
Shape of Data: (1017209, 44)
Distinct Datatypes: [dtype('int64') dtype('O')
dtype('float64')]
```

As you can see, the shape of the data looks good with the new one-hot encoded form of data, but there is at least one column that has object as the data type within our dataframe. Let's check which column is still pending for data treatment.

```
print(temp.columns[temp.dtypes=="object"])
```

Output

```
Index(['StateHoliday'], dtype='object')
```

We can see that there is just one column that we missed for data treatment. Let's have a look at the contents of the feature before converting it to numeric or one-hot encoded form.

```
temp["StateHoliday"].unique()
```

Output

```
array(['0', 'a', 'b', 'c', 0], dtype=object)
```

The feature seems to have incorrect values. Ideally, StateHoliday should have either a 0 or 1 as the possible values to indicate whether it is a holiday or not. Let's repair the feature by replacing all values of "a," "b," and "c" with 1 and the rest with 0, therefore converting the variable as numeric.

```
temp["StateHoliday"]= np.where(temp["StateHoliday"]== '0',0,1)
#One last check of the data type
temp.dtypes.unique()
```

Output

```
array([dtype('int64'), dtype('float64')], dtype=object)
```

Now that we have all columns in the integer form, let's proceed to build our training and test datasets. As discussed earlier, we should divide train, validation, and test datasets in a ratio of 60:20:20. Given that we have a fairly large training dataset, we reduce the size of validation if required to keep the majority for training. This step is not necessary, but it is an option.

We will first create train and test datasets with an 80:20 ratio. Then, we will use the train dataset to further split into training and validation datasets at a 90:10 ratio. These ratios can be further adjusted based on your judgment. We can use the train_test_split function provided by the scikit-learn package to divide the datasets.

```
from sklearn.cross_validation import train_test_split
#Create train and test dataset with an 80:20 split
```

```
x_train, x_test, y_train, y_test = train_test_split(temp,
df_new[target],test_size=0.2,random_state=2018)
#Further divide training dataset into train and validation
dataset with an 90:10 split
x_train, x_val, y_train, y_val = train_test_split(x_train,
y_train,test_size=0.1,random_state=2018)

#Check the sizes of all newly created datasets
print("Shape of x_train:",x_train.shape)
print("Shape of x_val:",x_val.shape)
print("Shape of x_test:",x_test.shape)
print("Shape of y_train:",y_train.shape)
print("Shape of y_val:",y_val.shape)
print("Shape of y_test:",y_test.shape)
```

Output

```
Shape of x_train: (732390, 44)
Shape of x_val: (81377, 44)
Shape of x_test: (203442, 44)
Shape of y_train: (732390, 1)
Shape of y_val: (81377, 1)
Shape of y_test: (203442, 1)
```

The shapes of all the required datasets look to be in good shape. Now that we have the dataset in the required form for the model development and training, we need to design the DNN architecture. Unlike the previous small networks, we now need improved architectures for the model to appropriately learn and predict. Also, we will later need to measure the model performance and validate if it is performing well.

How do we determine whether our model is performing well?

This is an important question to tackle even before we begin designing the model performance. For each model we will develop, we will need to create a baseline score as the bare minimum score to consider the model useful. In most cases, we assume what predictions can be made without a model. For a regression model, if we assume the mean value of sales in the training dataset to be the prediction for all samples in the test dataset, we would have a basic benchmark score. The DL model should at least score better than this score to be considered as useful.

Defining Model Baseline Performance

To define the model baseline performance, we should consider the mean of the target variable in the training dataset as the prediction for all test samples. The metric we shall use to perform this test is MAE (mean absolute error).

```
#calculate the average score of the train dataset
mean_sales = y_train.mean()
print("Average Sales :",mean_sales)
```

Output

```
Average Sales : Sales      5773.099997
dtype: float64
```

Now, if we assume the average sales as the prediction for all samples in the test dataset, what does the MAE metric look like?

```
#Calculate the Mean Absolute Error on the test dataset
print("MAE for Test Data:",abs(y_test - mean_sales).mean()[0])
```

Output

```
MAE for Test Data: 2883.587604303215
```

So, our baseline performance is 2,883.58.

If our DL model doesn't deliver results better (i.e., lower) than the baseline score, then it would barely add any value.

Designing the DNN

While designing a DNN, we need to consider a few important aspects. We have limited computing power and time, so the luxury of testing all possible combinations of architectures is simply ruled out. DL models consume significantly larger amounts of data and computing time for training. We need to judiciously design network architectures that can learn as quickly as possible.

Here are a few guidelines.

- **Rule 1: Start with small architectures.**

  In the case of DNNs, it is always advised to start with a single-layer network with around 100–300 neurons. Train the network and measure performance using the defined metrics (while defining the baseline score). If the results are not encouraging, try adding one more layer with the same number of neurons and repeating the process.

- **Rule 2: When small architectures (with two layers) fail, increase the size.**

  When the results from small networks are not great, you need to increase the number of neurons in layers by three to five times (i.e., around 1,000 neurons in each layer). Also, increase regularization (to be covered in depth in Chapter 5) to 0.3, 0.4, or 0.5 for both layers and repeat the process for training and performance measurement.

- **Rule 3: When larger networks with two layers fail, go deeper.**

  Try increasing the depth of the network with more and more layers while maintaining regularization with dropout layers (if required) after each dense (or your selected layer) with a dropout rate between 0.2 and 0.5.

- **Rule 4: When larger and deeper networks also fail, go even larger and even deeper.**

  In case large networks with ~1000 neurons and five or six layers also don't give the desired performance, try increasing the width and depth of the network. Try adding layers with 8,000–10,000 neurons per layer and a dropout of 0.6 to 0.8.

- **Rule 5: When everything fails, revisit the data.**

  If all the aforementioned rules fail, revisit the data for improved feature engineering and normalization, and then you will need to try other ML alternatives.

So, let's get started. The following code snippet creates a DNN with just one layer of 150 neurons.

```
#Create Deep Neural Network Architecture
from keras.models import Sequential
from keras.layers import Dense, Dropout

model = Sequential()
model.add(Dense(150,input_dim = 44,activation="relu"))
#The input_dim =44, since the width of the training data=44
(refer data engg section)
model.add(Dense(1,activation = "linear"))
```

```
#Configure the model
model.compile(optimizer='adam',loss="mean_absolute_error",
metrics=["mean_absolute_error"])

#Train the model
model.fit(x_train.values,y_train.values, validation_data=
(x_val,y_val),epochs=10,batch_size=64)
```

Output

```
Train on 732390 samples, validate on 81377 samples
Epoch 1/10
732390/732390 [==============================] - 14s 19us/
step - loss: 2484443.9857 - mean_absolute_error: 982.3168 -
val_loss: 1705817.0064 - val_mean_absolute_error: 866.8005
Epoch 2/10
732390/732390 [==============================] - 15s 20us/
step - loss: 1556789.8048 - mean_absolute_error: 851.0444 -
val_loss: 1513560.3941 - val_mean_absolute_error: 880.7449
Epoch 3/10
732390/732390 [==============================] - 14s 19us/
step - loss: 1365229.7217 - mean_absolute_error: 823.4470 -
val_loss: 1354828.9200 - val_mean_absolute_error: 843.5079
Epoch 4/10
732390/732390 [==============================] - 15s 20us/
step - loss: 1264298.7544 - mean_absolute_error: 800.4497 -
val_loss: 1176297.4208 - val_mean_absolute_error: 775.9128
Epoch 5/10
732390/732390 [==============================] - 14s 20us/
step - loss: 1191949.2337 - mean_absolute_error: 776.4975 -
val_loss: 1118038.9334 - val_mean_absolute_error: 754.8027
Epoch 6/10
```

```
732390/732390 [==============================] - 15s 21us/
step - loss: 1145511.8379 - mean_absolute_error: 757.7596 -
val_loss: 1077273.3024 - val_mean_absolute_error: 737.5510
Epoch 7/10
732390/732390 [==============================] - 15s 21us/
step - loss: 1115707.3112 - mean_absolute_error: 744.6207 -
val_loss: 1110957.5719 - val_mean_absolute_error: 747.7849
Epoch 8/10
732390/732390 [==============================] - 14s 19us/
step - loss: 1096126.8665 - mean_absolute_error: 734.5611 -
val_loss: 1056226.5925 - val_mean_absolute_error: 721.077873 -
ETA: 0s - loss: 1096330.8107 - mean_absolute_error: 73
Epoch 9/10
732390/732390 [==============================] - 14s 20us/
step - loss: 1077081.6034 - mean_absolute_error: 723.8428 -
val_loss: 1043093.3088 - val_mean_absolute_error: 712.8212an_
absolute_error: 7
Epoch 10/10
732390/732390 [==============================] - 14s 19us/
step - loss: 1064185.7429 - mean_absolute_error: 715.7054 -
val_loss: 1028792.2388 - val_mean_absolute_error: 697.6917
```

The preceding output is showcased in progression as the model trains the DNN. It takes a batch of 64 training samples in an iteration, passes each sample through the network, and measures the loss metric that we defined. It uses the optimization technique we configured to update the model weights and repeats till the last batch for one epoch. The entire process is repeated ten times, since we set number of epochs as ten. At the end of each epoch, the model uses the validation dataset to evaluate and report the metrics we configured.

From the initial results, we can see a positive performance. The model performance on the validation dataset was 697, which is way better than our baseline score.

Testing the Model Performance

Let us now test the model performance on the test dataset.

```
#Use the model's evaluate method to predict and evaluate the
test datasets
result = model.evaluate(x_test.values,y_test.values)

#Print the results
for i in range(len(model.metrics_names)):
    print("Metric ",model.metrics_names[i],":",str(round(result
    [i],2)))
```

Output

```
203442/203442 [==============================] - 2s 10us/step
Metric  loss : 810.1835326664134
Metric  mean_absolute_error : 674.5
```

And there we go: we got a relatively consistent performance on the test dataset too.

Improving the Model

Let us now try further improving the model performance by experimenting with a couple of more complicated architectures. In the previous network, we used mean_absolute_error as the loss function. To improve learning in sync with our use case, we can use mean_squared_error. The squaring of the error helps to penalize higher error rates even more.

In the following network, we have added two more layers with similar numbers of neurons. We will update our loss function to mean squared error instead of MAE. Let's train the network and have a look at the performance on the test dataset.

```
model = Sequential()
model.add(Dense(150,input_dim = 44,activation="relu"))
model.add(Dense(150,activation="relu"))
model.add(Dense(150,activation="relu"))
model.add(Dense(1,activation = "linear"))

model.compile(optimizer='adam',loss="mean_squared_
error",metrics=["mean_absolute_error"])

history = model.fit(x_train,y_train, validation_data=(x_val,
y_val),epochs=10,batch_size=64)

#result = model.evaluate(x_test,y_test)
for i in range(len(model.metrics_names)):
    print("Metric ",model.metrics_names[i],":",str(round(result
    [i],2)))
```

Output

```
Train on 732390 samples, validate on 81377 samples
Epoch 1/10
732390/732390 [==============================] - 23s 32us/
step - loss: 1708038.6039 - mean_absolute_error: 848.4737 -
val_loss: 1138718.0817 - val_mean_absolute_error: 713.3368
Epoch 2/10
732390/732390 [==============================] - 23s 31us/
step - loss: 1145557.5467 - mean_absolute_error: 718.0267 -
val_loss: 1019385.8800 - val_mean_absolute_error: 679.1929
Epoch 3/10
```

```
732390/732390 [==============================] - 23s 31us/
step - loss: 1075842.6427 - mean_absolute_error: 695.9032 -
val_loss: 1066319.3633 - val_mean_absolute_error: 698.5687
Epoch 4/10
732390/732390 [==============================] - 23s 31us/
step - loss: 1053733.9089 - mean_absolute_error: 688.2615 -
val_loss: 996584.2376 - val_mean_absolute_error: 672.7340
Epoch 5/10
732390/732390 [==============================] - 23s 31us/
step - loss: 1028932.4075 - mean_absolute_error: 681.4085 -
val_loss: 963295.3702 - val_mean_absolute_error: 662.4607
Epoch 6/10
732390/732390 [==============================] - 23s 31us/
step - loss: 1004636.7859 - mean_absolute_error: 673.8713 -
val_loss: 985398.1829 - val_mean_absolute_error: 678.7933
Epoch 7/10
732390/732390 [==============================] - 24s 33us/
step - loss: 980104.8595 - mean_absolute_error: 667.2302 -
val_loss: 914751.1625 - val_mean_absolute_error: 651.7794
Epoch 8/10
732390/732390 [==============================] - 23s 32us/
step - loss: 963304.7831 - mean_absolute_error: 662.4571 -
val_loss: 955510.7847 - val_mean_absolute_error: 669.5784
Epoch 9/10
732390/732390 [==============================] - 23s 31us/
step - loss: 944079.1561 - mean_absolute_error: 656.3804 -
val_loss: 886288.1656 - val_mean_absolute_error: 639.5075
Epoch 10/10
732390/732390 [==============================] - 23s 31us/
step - loss: 924452.3857 - mean_absolute_error: 650.0512 -
val_loss: 911133.2878 - val_mean_absolute_error: 643.0542
```

```
203442/203442 [==============================] - 4s 19us/step
Metric  loss : 909847.03
Metric  mean_absolute_error : 638.72
```

We can see that as we created a deeper model, its performance on the test dataset improved further. The current result is much better than that from our previous model.

Let's try a couple of more experiments to see if we can expect further improved performance. We can develop another deeper model with five hidden layers having 150 neurons each. In this case, we have increased the number of epochs from 10 to 15. This would therefore increase computation.

```
model = Sequential()
model.add(Dense(150,input_dim = 44,activation="relu"))
model.add(Dense(150,activation="relu"))
model.add(Dense(150,activation="relu"))
model.add(Dense(150,activation="relu"))
model.add(Dense(150,activation="relu"))
model.add(Dense(1,activation = "linear"))

model.compile(optimizer='adam',loss="mean_squared_
error",metrics=["mean_absolute_error"])

model.fit(x_train,y_train, validation_data=(x_val,y_val),
epochs=15,batch_size=64)

result = model.evaluate(x_test,y_test)
for i in range(len(model.metrics_names)):
    print("Metric ",model.metrics_names[i],":",str(round(result
    [i],2)))
```

Output

```
732390/732390 [==============================] - 30s 41us/
step - loss: 1101835.3958 - mean_absolute_error: 702.2829 -
val_loss: 1010836.5122 - val_mean_absolute_error: 678.2764
```

--Skipping output for in between epochs--

```
Epoch 14/15
732390/732390 [==============================] - 30s 41us/
step - loss: 891425.8829 - mean_absolute_error: 635.5511 -
val_loss: 844685.8285 - val_mean_absolute_error: 620.1237
Epoch 15/15
732390/732390 [==============================] - 30s 41us/
step - loss: 883631.1386 - mean_absolute_error: 632.5584 -
val_loss: 871893.6526 - val_mean_absolute_error: 638.8337
203442/203442 [==============================] - 5s 23us/step
Metric  loss : 872514.05
Metric  mean_absolute_error : 635.84
```

We can now see a saturation point. The accuracy on the test dataset of 635.8; although this is a small improvement in the overall performance, it's not as much as we expected. Creating deeper networks might not be as useful for this size. Let us try increasing the number of neurons and starting with one or two layers.

Increasing the Number of Neurons

The following code snippet designs a neural network with two hidden layers having 350 neurons each and uses a model configuration similar to the previous architecture.

```
model = Sequential()
model.add(Dense(350,input_dim = 44,activation="relu"))
model.add(Dense(350,activation="relu"))
model.add(Dense(1,activation = "linear"))

model.compile(optimizer='adam',loss="mean_squared_
error",metrics=["mean_absolute_error"])
```

```
model.fit(x_train,y_train, validation_data=(x_val,y_val),
epochs=15,batch_size=64)

result = model.evaluate(x_test,y_test)
for i in range(len(model.metrics_names)):
    print("Metric ",model.metrics_names[i],":",
    str(round(result[i],2)))
```

Output

```
Train on 732390 samples, validate on 81377 samples
Epoch 1/15
732390/732390 [==============================] - 38s 52us/
step - loss: 1697413.8672 - mean_absolute_error: 854.0277 -
val_loss: 1467867.2202 - val_mean_absolute_error: 832.8275
Epoch 2/15
732390/732390 [==============================] - 39s 54us/
step - loss: 1154938.1155 - mean_absolute_error: 725.5312 -
val_loss: 1007847.0574 - val_mean_absolute_error: 685.1245
Epoch 3/15
732390/732390 [==============================] - 39s 53us/
step - loss: 1085253.5922 - mean_absolute_error: 700.4208 -
val_loss: 1050960.9477 - val_mean_absolute_error: 689.2257
```

--Skipping output for in between epochs--

```
Epoch 14/15
732390/732390 [==============================] - 44s 60us/
step - loss: 889136.7336 - mean_absolute_error: 637.8075 -
val_loss: 832445.6279 - val_mean_absolute_error: 621.5381
Epoch 15/15
732390/732390 [==============================] - 42s 57us/
step - loss: 883337.1976 - mean_absolute_error: 635.5014 -
val_loss: 844103.7393 - val_mean_absolute_error: 626.2723
```

```
203442/203442 [==============================] - 7s 33us/step
Metric  loss : 847824.59
Metric  mean_absolute_error : 623.83
```

We can see quite a bit of improvement when we use an architecture that was built with a higher number of neurons. This was a considerable improvement for the model. Let us now try deeper models for the same architecture. Additionally, we add a new [optional] configuration to the model to record the history of various metrics during the training process. This can be done by adding the callbacks parameter, as shown in the following example. We can use the history, post training, to visualize and understand the model's learning curve.

```
from keras.callbacks import History
history = History()

model = Sequential()
model.add(Dense(350,input_dim = 44,activation="relu"))
model.add(Dense(350,activation="relu"))
model.add(Dense(350,activation="relu"))
model.add(Dense(350,activation="relu"))
model.add(Dense(350,activation="relu"))
model.add(Dense(1,activation = "linear"))

model.compile(optimizer='adam',loss="mean_squared_
error",metrics=["mean_absolute_error"])

model.fit(x_train,y_train, validation_data=(x_val,y_val),
epochs=15,batch_size=64,callbacks=[history])

result = model.evaluate(x_test,y_test)

for i in range(len(model.metrics_names)):
    print("Metric ",model.metrics_names[i],":",str(round(result
    [i],2)))
```

Output

```
Train on 732390 samples, validate on 81377 samples
Epoch 1/15
732390/732390 [==============================] - 83s 113us/
step - loss: 1652045.7426 - mean_absolute_error: 842.9293 -
val_loss: 1176475.4327 - val_mean_absolute_error: 722.2341
Epoch 2/15
732390/732390 [==============================] - 78s 107us/
step - loss: 1166282.9895 - mean_absolute_error: 723.2949 -
val_loss: 1200598.2506 - val_mean_absolute_error: 741.1529
Epoch 3/15
732390/732390 [==============================] - 78s 107us/
step - loss: 1107753.5017 - mean_absolute_error: 704.6886 -
val_loss: 1014423.8244 - val_mean_absolute_error: 685.8464

    --Skipping output for in between epochs--

Epoch 14/15
732390/732390 [==============================] - 72s 99us/
step - loss: 867543.7561 - mean_absolute_error: 626.8261 -
val_loss: 909483.9017 - val_mean_absolute_error: 639.9942
Epoch 15/15
732390/732390 [==============================] - 84s 115us/
step - loss: 856165.2330 - mean_absolute_error: 622.1622 -
val_loss: 823340.0147 - val_mean_absolute_error: 614.6816
203442/203442 [==============================] - 12s 59us/step
Metric  loss : 825525.53
Metric  mean_absolute_error : 612.01
```

As you may have noticed, we have seen a further improvement in the overall test performance for the model with deeper architectures. We can keep exploring various architectures given the computation and training time we can afford for the experiments. I strongly encourage you to explore a couple of more DNN architectures to understand how performance varies.

Plotting the Loss Metric Across Epochs

The model also stores the history of a few important parameters and metrics we configured for the model. To see what the model training process looked like, we can plot the loss metric across epochs and see the amount of reduction the model achieved with each epoch.

The following code snippet showcases the training as well as the validation loss across epochs for the model.

```
plt.plot(history.history['loss'])
plt.plot(history.history['val_loss'])
plt.title("Model's Training & Validation loss across epochs")
plt.ylabel('Loss')
plt.xlabel('Epochs')
plt.legend(['Train', 'Validation'], loc='upper right')
plt.show()
```

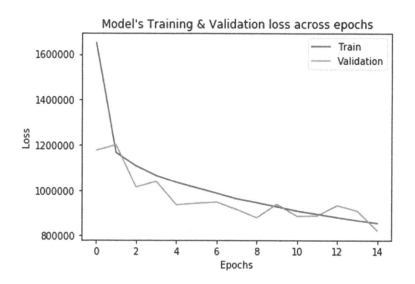

We can see that after a point the net decrease in loss was quite low but still relatively good. We could probably increase the number of epochs to test whether model performance is improving further. Of course, this comes with a significant amount of computation time for training, but once you have finalized the architecture for your model, you can increase the number of epochs for training and check if there was any further improvement.

Testing the Model Manually

We could also test the model's performance on the test dataset manually, instead of using the model's evaluate function. The following snippet calculates the model's mean squared error on the test dataset by using manual prediction on the test dataset.

```
#Manually predicting from the model, instead of using model's
evaluate function
y_test["Prediction"] = model.predict(x_test)
y_test.columns = ["Actual Sales","Predicted Sales"]
print(y_test.head(10))
```

```
#Manually predicting from the model, instead of using model's
evaluate function
from sklearn.metrics import mean_squared_error, mean_absolute_error
print("MSE :",mean_squared_error(y_test["Actual Sales"].
values,y_test["Predicted Sales"].values))
print("MAE :",mean_absolute_error(y_test["Actual Sales"].
values,y_test["Predicted Sales"].values))
```

Output

	Actual Sales	Predicted Sales
115563	0	0.103189
832654	0	0.103189
769112	2933	3073.666748
350588	8602	7848.280762
84435	9239	8838.069336
53018	0	0.103189
262419	0	0.103189
702267	5885	5651.779297
981431	0	0.103189

```
MSE : 825525.5321821237
MAE : 612.0117530558458
```

Summary

In this chapter, we have explored a supervised regression problem for DNN from end to end. We started with the problem statement and defined it using industry standard frameworks to get an intuitive understanding of why we are solving this problem. We then explored the data to understand the available features and different data types. We studied basic Python skills to help us ingest, manipulate, visualize, and transform data into the required form for DNNs. We then leveraged the building blocks of DNNs and Keras we saw in Chapter 2 to design, build, and iterate over various DL architectures. We saw how we can measure the performance and further improve it using DNNs.

In the next chapter, we will look at another business problem that we can solve using a DNN for classification in supervised learning.

## CHAPTER 4

Deep Neural Networks for Supervised Learning: Classification

In Chapter 3, we explored a DL use case for regression. We explored the entire problem-solving approach with a business-forward strategy. We leveraged all our learning from Chapters 1 and 2 in foundational DL and the Keras framework to develop DNNs for a regression use case. In this chapter, we will take our learning one step further and design a network for a classification use case. The approach overall remains the same, but there are a few nuances we need to keep in mind while solving a classification use case. Moreover, we will take our learning in this chapter one step ahead with extensive DNN architectures. Let's get started.

Getting Started

Similar to Chapter 3, we will consider Kaggle for our use case's data source. From the available options, we will use the dataset provided for the "Red Hat Business Value" competition. This competition was hosted on Kaggle a few years back, and the dataset is a really good business use case for our study. The archived competition is available at www.kaggle.com/c/predicting-red-hat-business-value. Just as in the previous use case, we need to read and accept the competition rules before downloading the dataset for our experiments. Once you have accepted the competition rules, you can download the dataset from the "Data" tab or www.kaggle. com/c/predicting-red-hat-business-value/data. The data will be downloaded as a zip file. After unzipping, you will have four different datasets. We will need only two of them: act_train.csv and people.csv.

You can copy these two datasets and keep them in a new folder for the current chapter's experiments. We will use the same environment for the use case, but before we begin, let's have a look at the problem statement and define the SCQ and the solution approach, just like we did in Chapter 3.

Problem Statement

The high-level problem statement is mentioned in the competition's description page. It highlights the problem that deals with predicting high-value customers for their business based on the operational interaction data and thereby helping the company effectively prioritize resources to generate more business and serve its customers better.

Let's have a look at the problem statement from a more business-centric view. We will start by understanding the customer better. The organization is an American multinational software company that provides open source software products to the enterprise community. Their primary product is Red Hat Enterprise Linux, the most popular distribution of Linux OS, used by various large enterprises. In its services, it helps organizations align their IT strategies by providing enterprise-grade solutions through an open business model and an affordable, predictable subscription model. These subscriptions from large enterprise customers create a substantial part of their revenue, and therefore it is of paramount importance for them to understand their valuable customers and serve them better by prioritizing resources and strategies to drive improved business value.

Designing the SCQ

The end stakeholder in this problem could be the sales team or the business development team; both of these teams are at the forefront of the company's operations to provide the best of services to their most valued customers. To achieve this objective more effectively, the business development team has now explored a data-driven solution to the problem. Given the vast operational interaction data and several customer attributes, they want to develop data-driven techniques to predict potential high-value customers for the business. With this context, let us now draft the SCQ for the business problem, just like we did for the regression use case in Chapter 3.

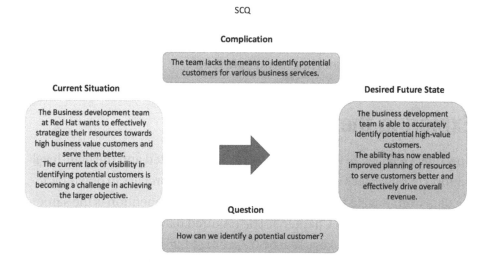

SCQ

Complication

The team lacks the means to identify potential customers for various business services.

Current Situation

The Business development team at Red Hat wants to effectively strategize their resources towards high business value customers and serve them better. The current lack of visibility in identifying potential customers is becoming a challenge in achieving the larger objective.

Desired Future State

The business development team is able to accurately identify potential high-value customers. The ability has now enabled improved planning of resources to serve customers better and effectively drive overall revenue.

Question

How can we identify a potential customer?

Designing the Solution

The SCQ showcased in the preceding illustration clearly defines the current situation and the desired future situation, while elucidating the roadblocks and the question that needs an answer in order to overcome impediments in achieving the larger objective. To design the solution, we need to start with the key question and work backward.

How Can We Identify a Potential Customer?

Red Hat has been in existence for over 25 years. In the long stint of business, they have accumulated and captured a vast amount of data from customer interactions and their descriptive attributes. This rich source of data could be a gold mine of patterns that can help in identifying a potential customer by studying the vast and complex historical patterns in the interaction data.

With the ever-growing popularity and prowess of DL, we can develop a DNN that can learn from historic customer attributes and operational interaction data to understand the deep patterns and predict whether a new customer will potentially be a high-value customer for various business services.

Therefore, we will develop and train a DNN to learn the chances that a customer will be a potential high-value customer, using various customer attributes and operational interaction attributes.

Exploring the Data

Now that we have the business problem clearly drafted and the high-level solution in place, let's start exploring the data. The process to download the data from Kaggle for Red Hat Business Value competition is the same as showcased earlier in Chapter 3. The required datasets are available to download here: www.kaggle.com/c/predicting-red-hat-business-value/data. Please follow the five steps demonstrated in the previous chapter to download the data.

Now, let's open Jupyter Notebooks and create a new notebook for the current experiments.

```
#Import the necessary packages
import pandas as pd
import numpy as np
```

```
import matplotlib.pyplot as plt
import seaborn as sns
%matplotlib inline

#Import the 2 datasets provided in the Zip Folder
df = pd.read_csv("/Users/jojomoolayil/Book/Chapter4/Data/
act_train.csv")
people = pd.read_csv("/Users/jojomoolayil/Book/Chapter4/Data/
people.csv")

#Explore the shape of the datasets
print("Shape of DF:",df.shape)
print("Shape of People DF:",people.shape)
```

Output

```
Shape of DF: (2197291, 15)
Shape of People DF: (189118, 41)
```

A final line of code:

```
#Explore the contents of the first dataset
df.head()
```

Output

	people_id	activity_id	date	activity_category	char_1	char_2	char_3	char_4	char_5	char_6	char_7	char_8	char_9	char_10	outcome
0	ppl_100	act2_1734928	2023-08-26	type 4	NaN	NaN	NaN	NaN	NaN	NaN	NaN	NaN	NaN	type 76	0
1	ppl_100	act2_2434093	2022-09-27	type 2	NaN	NaN	NaN	NaN	NaN	NaN	NaN	NaN	NaN	type 1	0
2	ppl_100	act2_3404049	2022-09-27	type 2	NaN	NaN	NaN	NaN	NaN	NaN	NaN	NaN	NaN	type 1	0
3	ppl_100	act2_3651215	2023-08-04	type 2	NaN	NaN	NaN	NaN	NaN	NaN	NaN	NaN	NaN	type 1	0
4	ppl_100	act2_4109017	2023-08-26	type 2	NaN	NaN	NaN	NaN	NaN	NaN	NaN	NaN	NaN	type 1	0

We can see that the train data provided for the competition has over 2 million rows and 15 columns and the people dataset has around 190K rows and 41 columns. Exploring the contents of the training dataset, we can see that it mostly has customer interaction data but is completely anonymized. Given the confidentiality of customers and their attributes, the entire

105

data is anonymized, and this leaves us with little knowledge about its true nature. This is a common problem in data science. Quite often, the team that develops DL models faces the challenge of the data confidentiality of the end customer and is therefore provided only anonymized and sometimes encrypted data. This still shouldn't be a roadblock. It is definitely best to have a data dictionary and complete understanding of the dataset, but nevertheless, we can still develop models with the provided information.

The act_train.csv (henceforth to be addressed as Activity data) has many null data points. At a high level, the dataset captures customer activity and provides some activity attributes, a few customer attributes (which are shown as null in the preceding output), another categorical feature named 'char_10' that we don't know much about, and finally the outcome variable.

Let's have a look at how many nulls the activity data has.

```
#Calculating the % of Null values in each column for activity data
df.isnull().sum()/df.shape[0]
```

Output

```
people_id           0.000000
activity_id         0.000000
date                0.000000
activity_category   0.000000
char_1              0.928268
char_2              0.928268
char_3              0.928268
char_4              0.928268
char_5              0.928268
char_6              0.928268
char_7              0.928268
```

```
char_8                 0.928268
char_9                 0.928268
char_10                0.071732
outcome                0.000000
dtype: float64
```

Around nine features have more than 90% null values. We can't do much to fix these features. Let's move ahead and have a look at the people dataset.

```
#Explore the contents of People dataset
people.head()
```

Output

	people_id	char_1	group_1	char_2	date	char_3	char_4	char_5	char_6	char_7	...	char_29	char_30	char_31	char_32	char_33	char_34	char_35
0	ppl_100	type 2	group 17304	type 2	2021-06-29	type 5	type 5	type 5	type 3	type 11	...	False	True	True	False	False	True	True
1	ppl_100002	type 2	group 8688	type 3	2021-01-06	type 28	type 9	type 5	type 3	type 11	...	False	True	True	True	True	True	True
2	ppl_100003	type 2	group 33592	type 3	2022-06-10	type 4	type 8	type 5	type 2	type 5	...	False	False	True	True	True	True	False
3	ppl_100004	type 2	group 22593	type 3	2022-07-20	type 40	type 25	type 9	type 4	type 16	...	True	True	True	True	True	True	True
4	ppl_100006	type 2	group 6534	type 3	2022-07-27	type 40	type 25	type 9	type 3	type 8	...	False	False	True	False	False	False	True

We already know that the people dataset (henceforth to be addressed as customer data) has around 41 columns; when we into the contents (which are only partially displayed in the preceding illustration due to the large number of columns), we see that we are provided with a lot of customer attributes, though we can't make any sense out of them. Moreover, the column names are same as the ones in the activity data. We need to change them before joining to avoid name clashes.

Let's check how many missing data points the customer dataset has. Since the customer dataset has around 40+ features, we can combine the missing value percentages for all columns together with the preceding code, instead of looking at each column individually.

```
#Calculate the % of null values in for the entire dataset
people.isnull().sum().sum()
```

Output

0

And we see that none of the columns in the customer dataset has missing values.

To create a consolidated dataset, we need to join the activity and customer data on the people_id key. But before we do that, we need to take care of a few things. We need to drop the columns in the activity data that have 90% missing values, as they cannot be fixed. Secondly, the "date" and "char_10" columns are present in both datasets. In order to avoid a name clash, let us rename the "date" column in the activity dataset to "activity_date" and "char_10" in the activity data as "activity_type." Next, we also need to fix the missing values in the "activity_type" column. Once these two tasks are accomplished, we will join the two datasets and explore the consolidated data.

```
#Create the list of columns to drop from activity data
columns_to_remove = ["char_"+str(x) for x in  np.arange(1,10)]
print("Columns to remove:",columns_to_remove)
```

```
#Remove the columns from the activity data
df = df[list(set(df.columns) - set(columns_to_remove))]
```

```
#Rename the 2 columns to avoid name clashes in merged data
df = df.rename(columns={"date":"activity_
date","char_10":"activity_type"})
```

```
#Replace nulls in the activity_type column with the mode
df["activity_type"] = df["activity_type"].fillna(df["activity_
type"].mode()[0])
```

```
#Print the shape of the final activity dataset
print("Shape of DF:",df.shape)
```

Output

```
Columns to remove: ['char_1', 'char_2', 'char_3', 'char_4',
'char_5', 'char_6', 'char_7', 'char_8', 'char_9']

Shape of DF: (2197291, 6)
```

We can now join the two datasets to create a consolidate activity and customer attributes dataset.

```
#Merge the 2 datasets on 'people_id' key
df_new = df.merge(people,on=["people_id"],how="inner")
print("Shape before merging:",df.shape)
print("Shape after merging :",df_new.shape)
```

Output

```
Shape before merging: (2197291, 6)
Shape after merging : (2197291, 46)
```

The consistent number of rows and the increase in the number of columns helps us validate that the join operation worked as expected. Let us now study the target (i.e., the variable we want to predict), named "outcome" in the dataset. We can check the distribution between potential vs. nonpotential customers.

```
print("Unique values for outcome:",df_new["outcome"].unique())
print("\nPercentage of distribution for outcome-")
print(df_new["outcome"].value_counts()/df_new.shape[0])3
```

Outcome

```
Unique values for outcome: [0 1]
```

```
Percentage of distribution for outcome-
0    0.556046
1    0.443954
Name: outcome, dtype: float64
```

We can see that there is a good mix in the distribution of potential customers, as around 45% are potential customers.

Data Engineering

Next, given that we have 45 columns altogether to explore and transform, let's expedite the process by automating a few things. Let's have a look at the different data types in the consolidated dataframe.

```
#Checking the distinct datatypes in the dataset
print("Distinct DataTypes:",list(df_new.dtypes.unique()))
```

Output

```
Distinct DataTypes: [dtype('int64'), dtype('O'), dtype('bool')]
```

We have numeric, categorical (Object), and Boolean features in the dataset. Boolean in Python represents a True or False value; we need to convert this into numeric (1 and 0) for the model to process the data. The following snippet of code converts the Boolean columns in the dataframe into numeric (1 and 0)–based values.

```
#Create a temp dataset with the datatype of columns
temp = pd.DataFrame(df_new.dtypes)
temp.columns = ["DataType"]
#Create a list with names of all Boolean columns
```

```
boolean_columns = temp.index[temp["DataType"] == 'bool'].values

print("Boolean columns - \n",boolean_columns)

#Convert all boolean columns to Binary numeric values
for column in boolean_columns:
    df_new[column] = np.where(df_new[column] == True,1,0)

print("\nDistinct DataTypes after processing:",df.dtypes.
unique())
```

Output

```
Boolean columns -
['char_10"char_11"char_12"char_13"char_14"char_15"char_16'
 'char_17"char_18"char_19"char_20"char_21"char_22"char_23'
 'char_24"char_25"char_26"char_27"char_28"char_29"char_30'
 'char_31"char_32"char_33"char_34"char_35"char_36"char_37']
```

```
Distinct DataTypes after processing: [dtype('int64')
dtype('O')]
```

Let us now have a look at the categorical features. We will first do a sanity check to understand the number of distinct values in each of the categorical features. If there are categorical features where there are unusually high numbers of distinct values, we have to decide if we can really convert them to a one-hot encoded structure for further processing.

```
#Extracting the object columns from the above dataframe
categorical_columns = temp.index[temp["DataType"] == 'O'].
values
```

```
#Check the number of distinct values in each categorical column
for column in categorical_columns:
    print(column+" column has :",str(len(df_new[column].
    unique())))+" distinct values")
```

Output

```
activity_category column has : 7 distinct values
activity_id column has : 2197291 distinct values
people_id column has : 151295 distinct values
activity_type column has : 6516 distinct values
activity_date column has : 411 distinct values
char_1 column has : 2 distinct values
group_1 column has : 29899 distinct values
char_2 column has : 3 distinct values
date column has : 1196 distinct values
char_3 column has : 43 distinct values
char_4 column has : 25 distinct values
char_5 column has : 9 distinct values
char_6 column has : 7 distinct values
char_7 column has : 25 distinct values
char_8 column has : 8 distinct values
char_9 column has : 9 distinct values
```

The five highlighted columns as shown in the output have high numbers of distinct values. It would be difficult to convert them into a one-hot encoded form, as they will consume too much memory during processing. In case you have the luxury of surplus RAM, feel free to convert them to a one-hot encoded data form.

For now, we can have a look at the content in these categorical columns to understand the approach by which we can convert them into numeric. Also, the date and activity_date columns are date values; therefore, we can convert them into data-related features like we did in the previous chapter. Let's first fix the date-related columns and then huddle with the remaining categorical columns. The following code snippet converts the date values to new features and then deletes the actual column.

```python
#Create date related features for 'date' in customer data
df_new["date"] = pd.to_datetime(df_new["date"])

df_new["Year"] = df_new["date"].dt.year
df_new["Month"] = df_new["date"].dt.month
df_new["Quarter"] = df_new["date"].dt.quarter
df_new["Week"] = df_new["date"].dt.week
df_new["WeekDay"] = df_new["date"].dt.weekday
df_new["Day"] = df_new["date"].dt.day

#Create date related features for 'date' in activity data
df_new["activity_date"] = pd.to_datetime(df_new["activity_date"])

df_new["Activity_Year"] = df_new["activity_date"].dt.year
df_new["Activity_Month"] = df_new["activity_date"].dt.month
df_new["Activity_Quarter"] = df_new["activity_date"].dt.quarter
df_new["Activity_Week"] = df_new["activity_date"].dt.week
df_new["Activity_WeekDay"] = df_new["activity_date"].dt.weekday
df_new["Activity_Day"] = df_new["activity_date"].dt.day

#Delete the original date columns
del(df_new["date"])
del(df_new["activity_date"])

print("Shape of data after create Date Features:",df_new.shape)
```

Output

```
Shape of data after create Date Features: (2197291, 56)
```

Let us now have a look at the remaining categorical columns, which have very high numbers of distinct values.

```
print(df_new[["people_id","activity_type","activity_id",
"group_1"]].head())
```

Output

```
people_id activity_type   activity_id       group_1
0    ppl_100          type 76   act2_1734928   group 17304
1    ppl_100          type 1    act2_2434093   group 17304
2    ppl_100          type 1    act2_3404049   group 17304
3    ppl_100          type 1    act2_3651215   group 17304
4    ppl_100          type 1    act2_4109017   group 17304
```

It seems that we can convert all of the preceding categorical columns into numeric by extracting the relevant numeric ID from each of them, since each of these columns has values in the form of someText_ someNumber. Rather than converting these categorical columns into a bloated one-hot encoded dataset, we can temporarily use them as numeric features. However, if the performance of the model doesn't reach our desired expectations after several experiments, we might have to revisit these features and try our best to incorporate them differently. But for now, we can consider them as numeric features.

The following code snippet extracts the numeric portion of the columns and converts the columns from a string to a numeric feature.

```
#For people ID, we would need to extract values after '_'
df_new.people_id = df_new.people_id.apply(lambda x:x.split("_")[1])
df_new.people_id = pd.to_numeric(df_new.people_id)

#For activity ID also, we would need to extract values after '_'
```

```
df_new.activity_id = df_new.activity_id.apply(lambda
x:x.split("_")[1])
df_new.activity_id = pd.to_numeric(df_new.activity_id)

#For group_1 , we would need to extract values after "
df_new.group_1 = df_new.group_1.apply(lambda x:x.split("")[1])
df_new.group_1 = pd.to_numeric(df_new.group_1)

#For activity_type , we would need to extract values after "
df_new.activity_type = df_new.activity_type.apply(lambda
x:x.split("")[1])
df_new.activity_type = pd.to_numeric(df_new.activity_type)

#Double check the new values in the dataframe
print(df_new[["people_id","activity_type","activity_id",
"group_1"]].head())
```

Output

```
people_id  activity_type  activity_id  group_1
0      100.0            76   1734928.0    17304
1      100.0             1   2434093.0    17304
2      100.0             1   3404049.0    17304
3      100.0             1   3651215.0    17304
4      100.0             1   4109017.0    17304
```

We now have the Boolean columns converted to numeric and also the categorical columns with large numbers of distinct values also converted to numeric. (Just a note: this categorical-to-numeric conversion is not always possible.) Next, let's convert the remaining categorical columns, which have relatively low numbers of distinct values, to one-hot encoded form and render the final consolidated dataset.

```
from sklearn.preprocessing import LabelEncoder, OneHotEncoder

#Define a function that will intake the raw dataframe and the
column name and return a one hot encoded DF
def create_ohe(df, col):
    le = LabelEncoder()
    a=le.fit_transform(df_new[col]).reshape(-1,1)
    ohe = OneHotEncoder(sparse=False)
    column_names = [col+ "_"+ str(i) for i in le.classes_]
    return(pd.DataFrame(ohe.fit_transform(a),columns =column_names))

#Since the above function converts the column, one at a time
#We create a loop to create the final dataset with all features
target = ["outcome"]
numeric_columns = list(set(temp.index[(temp.DataType =="float64") |
            (temp.DataType =="int64")].values) - set(target))

temp = df_new[numeric_columns]
for column in categorical_columns:
    temp_df = create_ohe(df_new,column)
    temp = pd.concat([temp,temp_df],axis=1)

print("\nShape of final df after onehot encoding:",temp.shape)
```

Output

```
Shape of final df after onehot encoding: (2197291, 183)
```

We now have the final form of the dataset ready for the model development. In this exercise, we have converted and kept the date-related features, as they are in their numeric form and not converted into the one-hot encoded form. This choice is optional. I considered the size of the dataset, with ~180 columns, as large enough to start with. We will conduct a few basic experiments, and if we don't see good performance, we will then need to revisit the data. In such a scenario, we need to look at improved strategies for how we can extract the best information from the vast selection of features in the most memory- and computation-efficient way.

Finally, before we begin with the model development, we need to split our datasets into train, validation, and test, just as we did in Chapter 3 for the regression use case. The following code snippet leverages the "train_test_split" from the sklearn package in Python to split the final dataset created in the preceding into train and test, and then further divide the train into train and validation.

```python
from sklearn.model_selection import train_test_split

#split the final dataset into train and test with 80:20
x_train, x_test, y_train, y_test = train_test_split(temp,
df_new[target], test_size=0.2,random_state=2018)
#split the train dataset further into train and validation
with 90:10
x_train, x_val, y_train, y_val = train_test_split(x_train,
y_train, test_size=0.1, random_state=2018)

#Check the shape of each new dataset created
print("Shape of x_train:",x_train.shape)
print("Shape of x_test:",x_test.shape)
print("Shape of x_val:",x_val.shape)
print("Shape of y_train:",y_train.shape)
print("Shape of y_test:",y_test.shape)
print("Shape of y_val:",y_val.shape)
```

Output

```
Shape of x_train: (1582048, 183)
Shape of x_test: (439459, 183)
Shape of x_val: (175784, 183)
Shape of y_train: (1582048, 1)
Shape of y_test: (439459, 1)
Shape of y_val: (175784, 1)
```

For now, we have the training data in the desired form for building DL models for classification. We need to define a baseline benchmark that will help us set the threshold performance we should expect from our models for them to be considered useful and acceptable.

Defining Model Baseline Accuracy

In Chapter 3, while we were working with the regression use case, we defined the baseline accuracy by using the mean of the training dataset as the final prediction for all the values in the test dataset. However, in the classification use case, we need a slightly different approach.

For all supervised classification use cases, our target variable would be a binary or multiclass (more than two classes) outcome. In our use case, we have the outcome as either 0 or 1. To validate the usefulness of a model, we should compare the result to what would have happened if we never had a model. In that case, we would make the largest class as the prediction for all customers and check what the accuracy looks like.

If you remember, the target in our use case (i.e., the outcome variable) has a good distribution of 1's and 0's. Here is the distribution of the outcome variable between 1 and 0.

```
#Checking the distribution of values in the target
df_new["outcome"].value_counts()/df_new.shape[0]
```

Output

```
0    0.556046
1    0.443954
Name: outcome, dtype: float64
```

So, with the preceding distribution, we can say that if we do not have any model and make all predictions as 0 (the largest class)—that is, predicting that none of the customers are potential high-value customers—then we would end up with at least 55.6% accuracy either way. This is our baseline accuracy. If we build a model that delivers us an overall accuracy anywhere below our benchmark, then it would be of practically no use.

Designing the DNN for Classification

For this use case, we have somewhat larger datasets. The training process might be more time-consuming than that of the regression use case. To save our time and be able to quickly get a well-functioning architecture in place, we will use a simple strategy. We will start with just three epochs for each kind of network we will experiment with, and once we find promising results, we will retrain the best architecture with the desired number of epochs for improved results.

To start with, let's follow the same guideline for the architecture development that we learned in Chapter 3. That is, let's follow Rule 1: Start small.

The following code snippet builds a DNN with just one layer and 256 neurons. We have used `binary_crossentropy` (since this a binary classification problem) as the loss function and accuracy as the metric to monitor. For classification problems, we can use several other metrics available within Keras, but accuracy is simple and fairly straightforward to comprehend. We will train the network for just three epochs and keep monitoring the loss as well as the accuracy on the training and validation dataset. If we don't see promising results, we might have to try a new architecture.

```
from keras.models import Sequential
from keras.layers import Dense

#Design the deep neural network [Small + 1 layer]
model  = Sequential()
model.add(Dense(256,input_dim = x_train.shape[1],activation=
"relu"))
model.add(Dense(256,activation="relu"))
model.add(Dense(1,activation = "sigmoid")) #activation =
sigmoid for binary classification

model.compile(optimizer = "Adam",loss="binary_crossentropy",
metrics=["accuracy"])

model.fit(x_train,y_train, validation_data = (x_val,y_val),
epochs=3, batch_size=64)
```

Output

```
Using TensorFlow backend.
Train on 1582048 samples, validate on 175784 samples
Epoch 1/3
1582048/1582048 [==============================] - 112s 71us/
step - loss: 8.8505 - acc: 0.4449 - val_loss: 8.8394 -
val_acc: 0.4455
Epoch 2/3
1582048/1582048 [==============================] - 111s 70us/
step - loss: 8.8669 - acc: 0.4438 - val_loss: 8.8394 -
val_acc: 0.4455
Epoch 3/3
```

```
1582048/1582048 [==============================] - 110s 69us/
step - loss: 8.8669 - acc: 0.4438 - val_loss: 8.8394 -
val_acc: 0.4455
```

If you closely observe the results from the training output, you will
see that the overall accuracy for training as well as validation datasets was
around 0.44 (44%), which is way lower than our baseline accuracy. We can
therefore conclude that training this model further might not be a fruitful
idea.

Let's try a deeper network for the same number of neurons. So, we
keep everything the same but add one more layer with the same number of
neurons.

```
#Design the deep neural network [Small + 2 layers]
model  = Sequential()
model.add(Dense(256,input_dim = x_train.shape[1],activation=
"relu"))
model.add(Dense(256,activation="relu"))
model.add(Dense(1,activation = "sigmoid"))

model.compile(optimizer = "Adam",loss="binary_crossentropy",
metrics=["accuracy"])

model.fit(x_train,y_train, validation_data = (x_val,y_val),
epochs=3, batch_size=64)
```

Output

```
Train on 1582048 samples, validate on 175784 samples
Epoch 1/3
1582048/1582048 [==============================] - 124s 79us/
step - loss: 8.8669 - acc: 0.4438 - val_loss: 8.8394 -
val_acc: 0.4455
Epoch 2/3
```

```
1582048/1582048 [==============================] - 125s 79us/
step - loss: 8.8669 - acc: 0.4438 - val_loss: 8.8394 -
val_acc: 0.4455
Epoch 3/3
1582048/1582048 [==============================] - 124s 78us/
step - loss: 8.8669 - acc: 0.4438 - val_loss: 8.8394 -
val_acc: 0.4455
```

Again, as we can see, the initial results are not at all promising. The training and validation accuracy from the deeper network are not anywhere close to what we would expect. Instead of trying another deeper network with, say, three to five layers, let us try training with a bigger (medium-sized) network. We shall use a new architecture with just one layer but 512 neurons this time. Let us again train for three epochs and have a look at the metrics to check whether it is in line with what we would expect.

```
#Design the deep neural network [Medium + 1 layers]
model  = Sequential()
model.add(Dense(512,input_dim = x_train.shape[1],activation=
"relu"))
model.add(Dense(1,activation = "sigmoid"))

model.compile(optimizer = "Adam",loss="binary_crossentropy",
metrics=["accuracy"])

model.fit(x_train,y_train, validation_data = (x_val,y_val),
epochs=3, batch_size=64)
```

Output

```
Train on 1582048 samples, validate on 175784 samples
Epoch 1/3
1582048/1582048 [==============================] - 113s 71us/
step - loss: 8.8669 - acc: 0.4438 - val_loss: 8.8394 -
val_acc: 0.4455
```

```
Epoch 2/3
1582048/1582048 [==============================] - 112s 71us/
step - loss: 8.8669 - acc: 0.4438 - val_loss: 8.8394 -
val_acc: 0.4455
Epoch 3/3
1582048/1582048 [==============================] - 112s 71us/
step - loss: 8.8669 - acc: 0.4438 - val_loss: 8.8394 -
val_acc: 0.4455
```

The medium-sized network too returned disappointing results. The training and validation accuracy from the medium-sized network are not really close to what we would expect. Let's now try increasing the depth for the medium-sized network to see if the results improve.

```
#Design the deep neural network [Medium + 2 layers]
model  = Sequential()
model.add(Dense(512,input_dim = x_train.shape[1],
activation="relu"))
model.add(Dense(512,activation="relu"))
model.add(Dense(1,activation = "sigmoid"))

model.compile(optimizer = "Adam",loss="binary_crossentropy",
metrics=["accuracy"])

model.fit(x_train,y_train, validation_data = (x_val,y_val),
epochs=3, batch_size=64)
```

Output

```
Train on 1582048 samples, validate on 175784 samples
Epoch 1/3
1582048/1582048 [==============================] - 135s 86us/
step - loss: 7.1542 - acc: 0.5561 - val_loss: 7.1813 -
val_acc: 0.5545
```

```
Epoch 2/3
1582048/1582048 [==============================] - 134s 85us/
step - loss: 7.1534 - acc: 0.5562 - val_loss: 7.1813 -
val_acc: 0.5545
Epoch 3/3
1582048/1582048 [==============================] - 135s 85us/
step - loss: 7.1534 - acc: 0.5562 - val_loss: 7.1813 -
val_acc: 0.5545
```

We can see that the results have improved, but only by just a bit. We see an accuracy of around 55% for the training and validation datasets, but these results are again not great, though better than what we previously had.

Revisiting the Data

The initial attempts to build a model with decent results have failed. We can further increase the size and the depth of the network, but this would only marginally increase the network performance. As discussed earlier, we might have to consider improving the data for training. We have two primary options here. We have discussed both of these points during the course of Chapter 2's "Input Data" section and Chapter 3's "Exploring the Data" section. We can standardize the input data with a 'Standardscaler' or a 'Minmaxscaler' using Python's sklearn package's tools or we can explore the options to revisit the one-hot encoding exercise for the categorical features we encoded as numeric. From these two options, the easiest and the least time-consuming would be standardizing or normalizing the data.

Standardize, Normalize, or Scale the Data

If you recollect, in the "Input Data" section under 'Getting Started with DL in Keras" in Chapter 2, we discussed that it is a good practice to standardize or normalize the data before providing it as training data for the DL models. We didn't use this as an option in Chapter 3 for the regression use case, as the model performed well on the regular data. However, in our classification use case, we can see that the performance is very poor on the raw data. To improve our model performance, let us try standardizing our data. (Alternatively, you can normalize the data too.)

In standardization, we transform the data into a form where the mean is 0 and the standard deviation is 1. The distribution of the data in this form is a great input candidate for our neuron's activation function and therefore improves the ability to learn more appropriately.

In its simplest form, standardization can be explained by the following example using a dummy input dataset. We perform standard scaling; look at the transformed values, the mean, and its standard deviation; and finally inverse transform the output to its original form.

```
#Create a dummy input
dummy_input = np.arange(1,10)
print("Dummy Input = ",dummy_input)

from sklearn.preprocessing  import StandardScaler

#Create a standardscaler instance and fit the data
scaler = StandardScaler()
output = scaler.fit_transform(dummy_input.reshape(-1,1))

print("Output =\n ",list(output))
print("Output's Mean = ",output.mean())
print("Output's Std Dev = ",output.std())
print("\nAfter Inverse Transforming = \n",list(scaler.inverse_
transform(output)))
```

Output

```
Dummy Input =  [1 2 3 4 5 6 7 8 9]
Output =
[array([-1.54919334]), array([-1.161895]),
array([-0.77459667]),
array([-0.38729833]), array([0.]), array([0.38729833]),
array([0.77459667]), array([1.161895]), array([1.54919334])]

Output's Mean =  0.0

Output's Std Dev =  1.0

After Inverse Transforming =
[array([1.]), array([2.]), array([3.]), array([4.]),
array([5.]),
array([6.]), array([7.]), array([8.]), array([9.])]
```

Transforming the Input Data

To transform the input data for the development of the model, please note that we should only use the training data to fit the scaler transformation and use the same fitted object to transform the validation and test input data. The following code snippet uses the x_train dataset to fit and transform the scaled values for all three datasets (i.e., x_train and x_val as well as x_test).

```
from sklearn.preprocessing import StandardScaler

scaler = StandardScaler()
scaler.fit(x_train)

x_train_scaled = scaler.transform(x_train)
x_val_scaled = scaler.transform(x_val)
x_test_scaled = scaler.transform(x_test)
```

Now that we have the standard scaled datasets, we can provide this newly augmented data for training. Please note that we haven't made any transformations to the labels or the target.

DNNs for Classification with Improved Data

Let us now start with a medium-sized network to see if we get improved results. We will start with just three epochs.

```
from keras import Sequential
from keras.layers import Dense
model  = Sequential()
model.add(Dense(512,input_dim = x_train_scaled.
shape[1],activation="relu"))
model.add(Dense(1,activation = "sigmoid"))

model.compile(optimizer = "Adam",loss="binary_crossentropy",
metrics=["accuracy"])

model.fit(x_train_scaled,y_train, validation_data =
(x_val_scaled,y_val), epochs=3, batch_size=64)
```

Output

```
Train on 1582048 samples, validate on 175784 samples
Epoch 1/3
1582048/1582048 [==============================] - 109s 69us/
step - loss: 0.2312 - acc: 0.8994 - val_loss: 0.1894 -
val_acc: 0.9225
Epoch 2/3
1582048/1582048 [==============================] - 108s 68us/
step - loss: 0.1710 - acc: 0.9320 - val_loss: 0.1558 -
val_acc: 0.9387
```

```
Epoch 3/3
1582048/1582048 [==============================] - 108s 68us/
step - loss: 0.1480 - acc: 0.9444 - val_loss: 0.1401 -
val_acc: 0.9482
```

Now, there we go!

We can see the drastic improvement in the performance of the network in providing the standardized datasets. We have an almost 95% accuracy on the training and validation datasets. Let's use this model to evaluate the model performance on the test datasets we created earlier.

```
result = model.evaluate(x_test_scaled,y_test)
for i in range(len(model.metrics_names)):
    print("Metric ",model.metrics_names[i],":",
    str(round(result[i],2)))
```

Output

```
439459/439459 [==============================] - 34s 76us/step
Metric  loss : 0.1
Metric  acc : 0.96
```

We see great results on the test dataset. Let's try improving the architecture a bit and see. We can a medium-sized deeper network to see if the results are better than with the medium-sized network.

```
#Designing the Deep Neural Network [Medium - 2 Layers]
model  = Sequential()
model.add(Dense(512,input_dim = x_train_scaled.shape[1],
activation="relu"))
model.add(Dense(512,activation="relu"))
model.add(Dense(1,activation = "sigmoid"))
```

```
model.compile(optimizer = "Adam",loss="binary_crossentropy",
metrics=["accuracy"])
```

```
model.fit(x_train_scaled,y_train, validation_data = (x_val_scaled,
y_val),epochs=3, batch_size=64)
```

Output

```
Train on 1582048 samples, validate on 175784 samples
Epoch 1/3
1582048/1582048 [==============================] - 131s 83us/
step - loss: 0.1953 - acc: 0.9141 - val_loss: 0.1381 -
val_acc: 0.9421
Epoch 2/3
1582048/1582048 [==============================] - 130s 82us/
step - loss: 0.1168 - acc: 0.9529 - val_loss: 0.1051 -
val_acc: 0.9578
Epoch 3/3
1582048/1582048 [==============================] - 131s 83us/
step - loss: 0.0911 - acc: 0.9646 - val_loss: 0.0869 -
val_acc: 0.9667
```

The training and validation accuracy has improved even further to 96%. This small increase with just 3 epochs is awesome. We can now be confident of the performance for the model with the architecture. We can definitely try many more architectures and check the results, but let's take a final shot with a larger and deeper network and see the results with 3 epochs. In case we see only small improvements, we will use the same architecture for 15 epochs and use the model for our final predictions.

```
#Designing the network Deep Neural Network - [Large + 2 Layers]
model  = Sequential()
model.add(Dense(1024,input_dim = x_train_scaled.shape[1],
activation="relu"))
```

```
model.add(Dense(1024,activation = "relu"))
model.add(Dense(1,activation = "sigmoid"))

model.compile(optimizer = "Adam",loss="binary_crossentropy",
metrics=["accuracy"])

model.fit(x_train_scaled,y_train, validation_data =
(x_val_scaled,y_val),epochs=3, batch_size=64)
```

Output

```
Train on 1582048 samples, validate on 175784 samples
Epoch 1/3
1582048/1582048 [==============================] - 465s 294us/
step - loss: 0.2014 - acc: 0.9099 - val_loss: 0.1438 -
val_acc: 0.9390
Epoch 2/3
1582048/1582048 [==============================] - 483s 305us/
step - loss: 0.1272 - acc: 0.9469 - val_loss: 0.1184 -
val_acc: 0.9524
Epoch 3/3
1582048/1582048 [==============================] - 487s 308us/
step - loss: 0.1015 - acc: 0.9593 - val_loss: 0.1011 -
val_acc: 0.9605
```

We see an overall accuracy on the validation dataset as 96% and
a similar score for the training dataset. So, there really isn't a lot of
improvement in the performance of the model due to increasing the size
from a medium (512-neuron) to a larger (1024-neuron) architecture.
With these results validating our experiments, let's train a medium-sized
(512-neuron) deep network with two layers for 15 epochs, look at the
final training and validation accuracy, and then use the trained model to
evaluate the test datasets.

```
#Designing the network Deep Neural Network - [Medium + 2 Layers]
model  = Sequential()
model.add(Dense(512,input_dim = x_train_scaled.
shape[1],activation="relu"))
model.add(Dense(512,activation = "relu"))
model.add(Dense(1,activation = "sigmoid"))

model.compile(optimizer = "Adam",loss="binary_crossentropy",
metrics=["accuracy"])

model.fit(x_train_scaled,y_train, validation_data = (x_val_
scaled,y_val),epochs=15, batch_size=64)
```

Output

```
Train on 1582048 samples, validate on 175784 samples
Epoch 1/15
1582048/1582048 [==============================] - 133s 84us/
step - loss: 0.1949 - acc: 0.9142 - val_loss: 0.1375 -
val_acc: 0.9426
Epoch 2/15
1582048/1582048 [==============================] - 133s 84us/
step - loss: 0.1173 - acc: 0.9527 - val_loss: 0.1010 -
val_acc: 0.9599
Epoch 3/15
1582048/1582048 [==============================] - 133s 84us/
step - loss: 0.0911 - acc: 0.9643 - val_loss: 0.0887 -
val_acc: 0.9660
```

----Skipping output from intermediate epochs -----

```
Epoch 14/15
1582048/1582048 [==============================] - 133s 84us/step -
loss: 0.0402 - acc: 0.9863 - val_loss: 0.0614 - val_acc: 0.9821
Epoch 15/15
```

```
1582048/1582048 [==============================] - 133s 84us/
step - loss: 0.0394 - acc: 0.9869 - val_loss: 0.0629 -
val_acc: 0.9818
```

The final model with a medium-size architecture of 512 neurons and two layers gave great performance results on the training and validation datasets. We have an accuracy of ~98% for both datasets. Let us now validate the model performance on the test dataset.

```
result = model.evaluate(x_test_scaled,y_test)

for i in range(len(model.metrics_names)):
    print("Metric ",model.metrics_names[i],":",
    str(round(result[i],2)))
```

Output

```
439459/439459 [==============================] - 20s 45us/step
Metric   loss : 0.06
Metric   acc : 0.98
```

The performance on the unseen test dataset is also great and consistent. Our model is performing really well on the test dataset. Let us have a look at the loss curve for the model, just like we did for the regression use case. We will plot the loss in each epoch (15 in total for this mode) for the training and validation datasets. The following code snippet leverages the model history and plots these metrics.

```
import matplotlib.pyplot as plt
%matplotlib inline
plt.plot(model.history.history['loss'])
plt.plot(model.history.history['val_loss'])
plt.title("Model's Training & Validation loss across epochs")
plt.ylabel('Loss')
plt.xlabel('Epochs')
```

```
plt.legend(['Train', 'Validation'], loc='upper right')
plt.show()
```

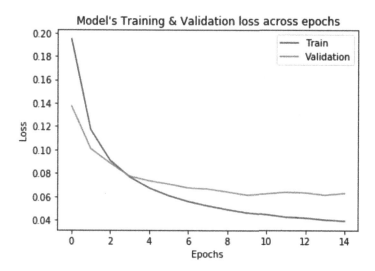

We can see decreasing loss across both datasets. Similarly, let's have a look at the accuracy metric during the model training. The accuracy metric for the training and validation datasets is also stored in the model history.

```
plt.plot(model.history.history['acc'])
plt.plot(model.history.history['val_acc'])
plt.title("Model's Training & Validation Accuracy across epochs")
plt.ylabel('Accuracy')
plt.xlabel('Epochs')
plt.legend(['Train', 'Validation'], loc='upper right')
plt.show()
```

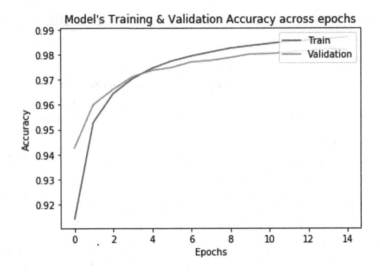

The accuracy, as we can see, has consistently increased with each epoch. In scenarios where we observe a huge gap between the training and the validation data for any metric, it would be an indication of an overfitting model. In such cases, the model performs very well on the training dataset but performs very poorly on the unseen data (i.e., validation as well as test dataset).

Summary

In this chapter, we have explored a business use case and solved it by leveraging a DNN for classification. We started by understanding the business essence of the problem statement, explored the provided data, and augmented into a suitable form for DNNs. We experimented with a few architectures, keeping in mind the rule of thumb we learned in Chapter 3, and we saw a major shortcoming in model performance. We then revisited the data and used standardization to represent the data in a more DL-friendly form and architecture for a few DNNs, and we saw amazing results. Overall, we reinforced our learning in data engineering, data exploration, DL, and with Keras and Python. In the next chapter, we will explore additional strategies to improve model performance with hyperparameter tuning, understand transfer learning, and explore a high-level process of model deployment for a large software.

CHAPTER 5

Tuning and Deploying Deep Neural Networks

So far in the journey of this book, we have primarily talked about how to develop a DNN for a given use case and looked at a few strategies and rules of thumb to bypass roadblocks we could face in the process. In this chapter, we will discuss the journey onward after developing the initial model by exploring the methods and approaches you need to implement when the model developed doesn't perform to your expectations. We will discuss regularization and hyperparameter tuning, and toward the end of the chapter, we will also have a high-level view of the process to deploy a model after tuning. However, we won't actually discuss the implementation specifics of deploying; this will just be an overview offering guidelines to achieve success in the process. Let's get started.

The Problem of Overfitting

In the process of developing and training ML and DL models, you will often come across a scenario where the trained model seems to perform well on the training dataset but fails to perform similarly on the test dataset. In data science, this phenomenon is called "overfitting." In a literal sense, your model overfits the data. Although you have crossed paths with this term previously in this book, we haven't discussed this topic in detail so far. Let's try to understand this phenomenon in a more simplified way.

© Jojo Moolayil 2019
J. Moolayil, *Learn Keras for Deep Neural Networks*,
https://doi.org/10.1007/978-1-4842-4240-7_5

The process of training a model is called "fitting the data"; the neural network learns the latent patterns within the data and mathematically improves the model weights/structure to suit the patterns it discovers in the learning process. In a nutshell, training the model adapts the its structure (weights) to fit the data (patterns) and thereby improves its performance. This beautiful process gets complicated at the point when the pattern it discovers turns out to be merely noise in reality. Unfortunately, the mathematical equation doesn't have the prowess to always distinguish between a signal and a noise (by noise, we mean a data point that doesn't represent the training sample but comes about due to random chance). When it fails, it learns the noise too and adjusts its weight to accommodate the new signal, which was noise in reality.

To understand this process, let's take a simple example. Say a five-year-old loves to eat cakes baked by his mother. He demands cakes to be baked every day at home. His mother politely denies these demands, but assures him that she will bake cakes on certain occasions. The little boy now looks forward to each new day, hoping that it will be one of those occasions when his mother will bake a cake. His mother, on the other hand, had no real intention to find occasions to bake cakes. She would simply bake a cake every Sunday when she had time off from work. The five-year-old continues to watch every day and slowly learns that his mom will bake a cake on every Sunday. So, he learns the following pattern: "If day == Sunday, then Mother will bake cakes." One fine Sunday, his mother had to travel for an errand and was left with no time to bake a cake. The five-year-old couldn't understand his pattern breaking down. So, to accommodate the new event, he modified his rules by formulating the new pattern as follows: "If day == Sunday, then Mother will bake a cake, but if the day is in the last week of the month, then no cake." In reality, the Sunday his mother missed baking the cake was a noise. He should have ideally ignored that and kept his previously learned pattern intact. But unfortunately, he failed to distinguish between signal and noise and thereby overcomplicated his rules and overfit the data.

Similarly, when a DL model learns from the noise and accommodates by adjusting the weights to suit the noise, it overfits the data. This problem becomes serious, since learning noise results in a significant decrease in model performance. That is the reason you would observe a large gap between the performance of a model on training data and the performance on unseen data. Circumventing this problem and tailoring a model's learning process to accommodate only signals (or real patterns) instead of noise can be achieved to a great extent (though not fully) with regularization.

So, What Is Regularization?

In simplest terms, regularization is a process to reduce overfitting. It is a mathematical way of inducing a warning into the model's learning process when it accommodates noise. To give a more realistic definition, it is a method to penalize the model weights in the event of overfitting.

Let's understand this process in a very simple way. In DL, the weights of the neuron connections are updated after each iteration. When the model encounters a noisy sample and assumes the sample is a valid one, it tries to accommodate the pattern by updating the weights aligned with the noise. In realistic data samples, noisy data points don't resemble anything close to a regular data point; they are far off from them. So, the weight updates will also be in sync with the noise (i.e., the change in weight will be huge). The process of regularization adds the weights of the edges to the defined loss function and holistically represents a higher loss. The network then tunes itself to reduce the loss and thereby makes the weight updates in the right direction; this works by ignoring the noise rather than accommodating it in the learning process.

The process of regularization can be demonstrated as

*Cost Function = **Loss** (as defined for the model) + **Hyperparameter** ×*
*[**Weights**]*

The hyperparameter is represented as $\dfrac{\lambda}{2m}$ and the value of λ is defined by the user.

Based on how the weights are added to the loss function, we have two different types of regularization techniques: L1 and L2.

L1 Regularization

In L1 regularization, the absolute weights are added to the loss function. To make the model more generalized, the values of the weights are reduced to 0, and therefore this method is strongly preferred when we are trying to compress the model for faster computation.

The equation can be represented as

$$\text{Cost Function} = \text{Loss (as defined)} + \frac{\lambda}{2m} * \sum \|Weights\|$$

In Keras, the L1 loss can be added to a layer by providing the 'regularizer' object to the 'kernel regularizer' parameter. The following code snippet demonstrates adding an L1 regularizer to a dense layer in Keras.

```
from keras import regularizers
from keras import Sequential

model = Sequential()
model.add(Dense(256, input_dim=128,
kernel_regularizer=regularizers.l1(0.01))
```

The value of 0.01 is the hyperparameter value we set for λ.

L2 Regularization

In L2 regularization, the squared weights are added to the loss function. To make the model more generalized, the values of the weights are reduced to near 0 (but not actually 0), and hence this is also called the "weight decay" method. In most cases, L2 is highly recommended over L1 for reducing overfitting.

The equation can be represented as

$$\text{Cost Function} = \text{Loss (as defined)} + \frac{\lambda}{2m} * \|Weights\|^2$$

We can add an L2 regularizer to a DL model just like L1. The following code snippet demonstrates adding an L2 regularizer to the dense layer.

```
model = Sequential()
model.add(Dense(256, input_dim=128,
kernel_regularizer=regularizers.l2(0.01))
```

The value of 0.01 is the hyperparameter value we set for λ.

Dropout Regularization

In addition to L1 and L2 regularization, there is another popular technique in DL to reduce overfitting. This technique is to use a dropout mechanism. In this method, the model arbitrarily drops or deactivates a few neurons for a layer during each iteration. Therefore, in each iteration the model looks at a slightly different structure of itself to optimize (as a couple of neurons and the connections would be deactivated). Say we have two successive layers, H1 and H2, with 15 and 20 neurons, respectively. Applying the dropout technique between these two layers would result in randomly dropping a few neurons (based on a defined percentage) for H1, which therefore reduces the connections between H1 and H2. This process repeats for each iteration with randomness, so if the model has learned for a batch and updated the weights, the next batch might have a fairly different set of weights and connections to train. The process is not only efficient due to the reduced computation but also works intuitively in reducing the overfitting and therefore improving the overall performance.

The idea of dropout can be visually understood using the following figure. We can see that the regular network has all neurons and connections between two successive layers intact. With dropout, each iteration induces a certain defined degree of randomness by arbitrarily deactivating or dropping a few neurons and their associated weight connections.

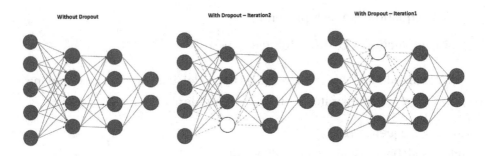

In Keras, we can use dropout to a layer with the following convention:

```
keras.layers.Dropout(rate, noise_shape=None, seed=None)
```

The following code snippet showcases dropout added to the dense hidden layer. The parameter value of 0.25 indicates the dropout rate (i.e., the percentage of the neurons to be dropped).

```
from keras import Sequential
from keras.layers.core import Dropout, Dense

model = Sequential()
model.add(Dense(100, input_dim= 50, activation='relu'))
model.add(Dropout(0.25))
model.add(Dense(1,activation="linear"))
```

Hyperparameter Tuning

Hyperparameters are the parameters that define a model's holistic structure and thus the learning process. We can also relate hyperparameters as the metaparameter for a model. It differs from a model's actual parameters, which it learns during the training process (say, the model weights). Unlike model parameters, hyperparameters cannot be learned; we need to tune them with different approaches to get improved performance.

To understand this topic better, let us look at the definition in a more simplified way. When we design a DNN, the architecture of the model is defined by a few high-level artifacts. These artifacts could be the number of neurons in a layer, the number of hidden layers, the activation function, the optimizer, the learning rate of the architecture, the number of epochs, batch size, and so on. All of these parameters are collectively used to design a network, and they have a huge impact on the model's learning process and its end performance. These parameters cannot be trained; in fact, they need to be selected with experience and judgment, just like the rules we learned in Chapter 3 to decide the size of the architecture to start with. Parameters that define the model's holistic architecture overall are collectively called hyperparameters. Choosing the right hyperparameters is an intensive and iterative process, but it becomes easier with experience. The process of experimenting with different values for hyperparameters to improve the overall model process is called model tuning or hyperparameter tuning.

Hyperparameters in DL

Let's have a look at the different hyperparameters available for a DL model and study the available options to choose from. We will then look at various approaches for selecting the right set of hyperparameters for a model.

Number of Neurons in a Layer

For most classification and regression use cases using tabular cross-sectional data, DNNs can be made robust by playing around with the width of the network (i.e., the number of neurons in a layer). Generally, a simple rule of thumb for selecting the number of neurons in the first layer is to refer to the number of input dimensions. If the final number of input dimensions in a given training dataset (this includes the one-hot encoded features also) is x, we should use at least the closest number to 2x in the power of 2. Let's say you have 100 input dimensions in your training dataset: preferably start with $2 \times 100 = 200$, and take the closest power of 2, so 256. It is good to have the number of neurons in the power of 2, as it helps the computation of the network to be faster. Also, good choices for the number of neurons would be 8, 16, 32, 64, 128, 256, 512, 1024, and so on. Based on the number of input dimensions, take the number closest to 2 times the size. So, when you have 300 input dimensions, try using 512 neurons.

Number of Layers

It is true that just adding a few more layers will generally increase the performance, at least marginally. But the problem is that with an increased number of layers, the training time and computation increase significantly. Moreover, you would need a higher number of epochs to see promising results. Not using deeper networks is not an always an option; in cases when you have to, try using a few best practices.

In case you are using a very large network, say more than 20 layers, try using a tapering size architecture (i.e., gradually reduce the number of neurons in each layer as the depth increases). So, if you are using an architecture of 30 layers with 512 neurons in each layer, try reducing the number of neurons in the layers slowly. An improved architecture would be with the first 8 layers having 512 neurons, the next 8 with 256, the next 8 with 128, and so on. For the last hidden layer (not the output layer), try keeping the number of neurons to at least around 30–40% of the input size.

Alternatively, if you are using wider networks (i.e., not reducing the number of neurons in the lower layers), always use L2 regularization or dropout layers with a drop rate of around 30%. The chances of overfitting are highly reduced.

Sample Tapering Network Architecture

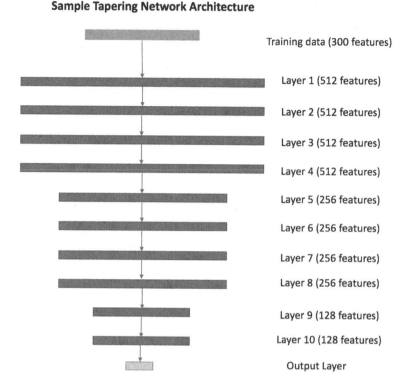

Training data (300 features)

Layer 1 (512 features)

Layer 2 (512 features)

Layer 3 (512 features)

Layer 4 (512 features)

Layer 5 (256 features)

Layer 6 (256 features)

Layer 7 (256 features)

Layer 8 (256 features)

Layer 9 (128 features)

Layer 10 (128 features)

Output Layer

Number of Epochs

Sometimes, just increasing the number of epochs for model training delivers better results, although this comes at the cost of increased computation and training time.

Weight Initialization

Initializing the weights for your network also has a tremendous impact on the overall performance. A good weight initialization technique not only speeds up the training process but also circumvents deadlocks in the model training process. By default, the Keras framework uses glorot uniform initialization, also called Xavier uniform initialization, but this can be changed as per your needs. We can initialize the weights for a layer using the kernel initializer parameter as well as bias using a bias initializer.

Other popular options to select are 'He Normal' and 'He Uniform' initialization and 'lecun normal' and 'lecun uniform' initialization. There are quite a few other options available in Keras too, but the aforementioned choices are the most popular.

The following code snippet showcases an example of initializing weights in a layer of a DNN with random_uniform.

```
from keras import Sequential
from keras.layers import Dense
model = Sequential()
model.add(Dense(64,activation="relu", input_dim = 32, kernel_
initializer = "random_uniform",bias_initializer = "zeros"))
model.add(Dense(1,activation="sigmoid"))
```

Batch Size

Using a moderate batch size always helps achieve a smoother learning process for the model. A batch size of 32 or 64, irrespective of the dataset size and the number of samples, will deliver a smooth learning curve in most cases. Even in scenarios where your hardware environment has large RAM memory to accommodate a bigger batch size, I would still recommend staying with a batch size of 32 or 64.

Learning Rate

Learning rate is defined in the context of the optimization algorithm. It defines the length of each step or, in simple terms, how large the updates to the weights in each iteration can be made. Throughout this book, we have ignored setting or changing the learning rate, as we have used the default values for the respective optimization algorithms, in our case Adam. The default value is 0.001, and this is a great choice for most scenarios. However, in some special cases, you might cross paths with a use case where it might be better to go with a lower learning rate or maybe slightly higher.

Activation Function

We have a generous choice of activation functions for the neurons. In most cases, ReLU works perfectly. You could almost always go ahead with ReLU as an activation for any use case and get favorable results. In cases where ReLU might not be delivering great results, experimenting with PReLU is a great option.

Optimization

Similar to activation functions, we also have a fairly generous number of choices available for the optimization algorithm of the network. While the most recommended is Adam, in scenarios where Adam might not be delivering the best results for your architecture, you could explore Adamax as well as Nadam optimizers. Adamax has mostly been a better choice for architectures that have sparsely updated parameters like word embeddings, which are mostly used in natural language processing techniques. We have not covered these advanced topics in the book, but it is good to keep these points in mind while exploring various architectures.

Approaches for Hyperparameter Tuning

So far, we have discussed various hyperparameters that are available for our DL models and also studied the most recommended options for generic situations. However, selecting the most appropriate value for a hyperparameter based on the data and the type of problem is more of an art. The art is also arduous and painfully slow. The process of hyperparameter tuning in DL is almost always slow and resource intensive. However, based on the style of selecting a value for hyperparameter and further tuning model performance, we can roughly divide the different types of approaches into four broad categories:

- Manual Search
- Grid Search
- Random Search
- Bayesian Optimization

Out of the four aforementioned approaches, we will have a brief look into the first three. Bayesian optimization is altogether a long and difficult topic that is beyond the scope for our book. Let's have a brief look at the first three approaches.

Manual Search

Manual search, as the name implies, is a completely manual way of selecting the best candidate value for the desired hyperparameters in a DL model. This approach requires phenomenal experience in training networks to get the right set of candidate values for all desired hyperparameters using the least number of experiments. Often this approach is highly efficient, provided you have sound experience in using them. The best approach to start with manual search is simply to leverage all the recommended values for a given hyperparameter and then to start training the network. The results may not be the best, but would definitely not be the worst. It's a good starting point for any newbie in the field to experiment with a few lowest-risk hyperparameter candidates.

Grid Search

In the grid search approach, you literally experiment with all possible combinations for a defined set of values of a hyperparameter. The name "grid" is actually derived from the gridlike combinations for the provided values of each hyperparameter. The following is a sample view of how a logical grid would look for three hyperparameters with three distinct values in each.

		Learning Rate			Optimizer			batch_size		
		0.1	0.01	0.001	Adam	Nadam	Adamax	32	64	128
Learning Rate	0.1				x	x	x	x	x	x
	0.01				x	x	x	x	x	x
	0.001				x	x	x	x	x	x
Optimizer	Adam	x	x	x				x	x	x
	Nadam	x	x	x				x	x	x
	Adamax	x	x	x				x	x	x
batch_size	32	x	x	x	x	x	x			
	64	x	x	x	x	x	x			
	128	x	x	x	x	x	x			

The approach is to try to develop a model for each of the combinations as shown in the preceding. The "x" indicates a model that will be developed with that particular hyperparameter value. For example, for learning rate (0.1), the vertical column shows the different models that will be developed with different values for optimizer and the batch size. Similarly, if you take a look at the horizontal row for the hyperparameter "batch-size" = 32, the "x" in all cells in the row indicates the different models that will be developed with different learning rate and optimizer values. So, in a grid with just three hyperparameters and three values each, we are looking at developing too many models. This process will be painfully long if we are developing fairly large networks and using larger training data samples.

The advantage of this approach is that it gives the best model for the defined grid of hyperparameters. However, the downside is that if your grid doesn't have great selections, your model will also not be the best one. It is simply assumed that the scientist working on the model has a fair idea of which ones could possibly be the best candidates for a given hyperparameter.

Keras doesn't directly provide the means to perform grid search tuning on the models. We can however use a custom for loop with the defined values for training or alternatively use the sklearn wrapper provided by Keras to package the model in an sklearn type object and then leverage the grid search method in sklearn to accomplish the results. The following code snippet showcases the means to use grid search from the sklearn package by using the Keras wrapper for a dummy model.

```
from keras import Sequential
from sklearn.model_selection import GridSearchCV
from keras.wrappers.scikit_learn import KerasClassifier
from keras.layers import Dense
import numpy as np

#Generate dummy data for 3 features and 1000 samples
x_train = np.random.random((1000, 3))

#Generate dummy results for 1000 samples: 1 or 0
y_train = np.random.randint(2, size=(1000, 1))

#Create a python function that returns a compiled DNN model
def create_dnn_model():
    model = Sequential()
    model.add(Dense(12, input_dim=3, activation='relu'))
    model.add(Dense(1, activation='sigmoid'))
    model.compile(loss='binary_crossentropy', optimizer='adam',
    metrics=['accuracy'])
    return model

#Use Keras wrapper to package the model as an sklearn object
model = KerasClassifier(build_fn=create_dnn_model)

# define the grid search parameters
batch_size = [32,64,128]
epochs = [15, 30, 60]

#Create a list with the parameters
param_grid = {"batch_size":batch_size, "epochs":epochs}
#Invoke the grid search method with the list of hyperparameters
```

```
grid_model = GridSearchCV(estimator=model, param_grid=param_
grid, n_jobs=-1)
#Train the model
grid_model.fit(x_train, y_train)

#Extract the best model grid search
best_model = grid_model.best_estimator_
```

Random Search

An improved alternative to grid search is random search. In a random
search, rather than selecting a value for the hyperparameter from a defined
list of numbers, like learning rate, we can instead choose randomly from a
distribution. This is, however, only possible for numeric hyperparameters.
So, instead of trying a learning rate of 0.1, 0.01, or 0.001, it can alternatively
pick up a random value for learning rate from a distribution we define
with some properties. The parameter now has a larger range of values
to experiment with and also much higher chances of getting better
performance. It overcomes the disadvantage of a human guessing the
best value for the hyperparameter confined within the defined range
by inducing randomness to bring the chance for better hyperparameter
selection. In reality, for most practical cases, random search mostly
outperforms grid search.

Further Reading

To explore some more concrete examples and a brief guide toward
Bayesian Optimization, please refer the following:

- https://towardsdatascience.com/a-conceptual-
  explanation-of-bayesian-model-based-
  hyperparameter-optimization-for-machine-
  learning-b8172278050f

- https://blog.floydhub.com/guide-to-
  hyperparameters-search-for-deep-learning-
  models/

Model Deployment

Now, we can finally discuss a few important pointers on model
deployment. We started with learning Keras and DL, experimented with
actual DNNs for regression and classification, and then discussed tuning
hyperparameters for improved model performance. We can now discuss a
few guidelines for deploying a DL model in a production environment.
I want to clarify that we won't actually be learning the process of deploying
a model in production as a software engineer or discuss the DL software
pipeline and architecture for a large enterprise project. We will instead
focus on a couple of important aspects to be kept in mind while deploying
the actual model.

Tailoring the Test Data

Throughout the course of this book, we have seen the test data exactly in
sync with the train data. In this book and for that matter in any ML/DL
learning guide, the experiments will always have the test data ready before
model training begins. We generally split the existing data into train and
test samples and then use the test data at our end to validate the model's
real performance. This is a fair process as long as your objective ends with
training and developing a model. Once your trained model goes live in a
software, you don't really have access to the test data. To actually make
use of the model, the data needs to be tailored in the expected format
so that the model can predict and return the predictions. This process is
actually arduous and requires carefully designing the data wrangling and
transformation pipeline for production software.

Let's understand this process with an example. Assume that you have designed and developed a DNN to predict a credit card transaction as "genuine" or "fraudulent" using a supervised classification model. While developing the model, you have access to customer data, transactions, point-of-sale attributes, time-related attributes, geographical attributes, and so on. All these data points exist in different sources. For development of the model, you would make the effort to get the data from these different sources and bring it in a unified form. For your experiment, this would actually be a one-time effort. In reality, once the model is live, this entire process needs to be designed in a way that it can replicate the ingestion of data for a given customer along with all other necessary attributes from different sources, unify and transform it into the required form for the model to predict, and then make inferences at scale. Think about a large bank, where the real-time application is catering to thousands of transactions at the same time across the globe. Getting the data tailored for inferencing from the model requires really sound engineering principles to enable the model to work without glitches.

The design principles of setting up the database or a cluster/node that will compute the query request in real time need to consider the data engineering and transformations that you have done on your training dataset, because that exact same process needs to be executed every time a prediction is supposed to be made using the model. This process of tailoring the data on the fly to make inferences is a totally different art on its own and requires careful engineering to build up. Usually, data scientists are least worried about this part of the puzzle. We dispose of it under the assumption that it is a software and data engineer's job and that we can just stop bothering with it. This myth will eventually be exploded, as there is a serious harmony that needs to be established to get this part of the puzzle in place. The two teams, namely, data scientists and software engineers, need to work hand in hand to accomplish this task. The difficulty faced by a data scientist in understanding a software engineer's requirements and vice versa led to the rise of a new role in the industry called ML engineer. An ML engineer is a candidate who has a great understanding of the intersection of the two fields.

Saving Models to Memory

Another useful point we didn't discuss during the course of this chapter is saving the model as a file into memory and reusing it at some other point in time. The reason this becomes extremely important in DL is the time consumed in training large models. You shouldn't be surprised when you encounter DL engineers who have been training models for weeks at a stretch on a supercomputer. Modern DL models that encompass image, audio, and unstructured text data consume a significant amount of time for training. A handy practice in such scenarios would be to have the ability to pause and resume training for a DL model and also save the intermediate results so that the training performed up to a certain point of time doesn't go to waste. This can be achieved with a simple callback (a procedure in Keras that can be applied to the model at different stages of training) that would save the weights of the model to a file along with the model structure after a defined milestone. This saved model can later be imported again whenever you want to resume the training. The process continues just like you would want it to. All we need to do is take care of saving the model structure as well as the weights after an epoch or when we have the best model in place. Keras provides the ability to save models after every epoch or save the best model during training for multiple epochs.

An example of saving the best weights of a model during training for a large number of epochs is shown in the following snippet.

```
from keras.callbacks import ModelCheckpoint

filepath = "ModelWeights-{epoch:.2f}-{val_acc:.2f}.hdf5"
checkpoint = ModelCheckpoint(filepath, save_best_only=True,
monitor="val_acc")

model.fit(x_train, y_train, callbacks=[checkpoint],epochs=100,
batch_size=64)
```

As you can see in this code snippet, we define a `callbacks` object with the desired parameters. We define when to save the model and what metric to measure and where to save the model. The file path uses a naming convention where it stores the model weights into a file with the file name depicting the epoch number and the corresponding accuracy metric. Finally, the `callbacks` object is passed into the model fit method as a list.

Alternatively, you can also save a model in its entire form after finishing training using the `save_model` method and later load it into memory (maybe the next day) using the `load_model` method. An example is shown in the following code snippet.

```
from keras.models import load_model
#Train a model for defined number of epochs
model.fit(x_train, y_train, epochs=100, batch_size=64)

# Saves the entire model into a file named as  'dnn_model.h5'
model.save('dnn_model.h5')

# Later, (maybe another day), you can load the trained model
for prediction.
model = load_model('dnn_model.h5')
```

Retraining the Models with New Data

When you deploy your model into production, the ecosystem will continue to generate more data, which can be used for training your models again. Say, for the credit card fraud use case, you trained your model with 100K samples and got a performance of 93% accuracy. You feel the performance is good enough to get started, so you deploy your model into production. Over a period of one month, an additional 10K samples are available from the new transactions made by customers. Now you would want your model to leverage this newly available data and improve its performance even further. To achieve this, you don't need to retrain the entire model again; you could instead use the pause-and-resume approach. All you need to do is use the weights of the model already trained and provide additional data with a few epochs to pass and iterate over the new samples. The weights it has already learned don't need to be disposed; you can simply use the pause-and-resume formula and continue with the incremental data.

Online Models

An immediate question you may ponder after understanding the process of retraining the model is how frequently should you do this: is it a good approach to retrain every day, every week, or every month? The right answer is to retrain as frequently as you want. There is no harm in incrementally training your models every time a new data point is available as long as the computation required is not a bottleneck. A good practice would be to iterate a training instance as soon as a new batch of samples is available. So, if you have set a `batch_size` of 64, you could automate the model training to ingest the newly available batch of data and further improve performance on future predictions by automating the software infrastructure to train the model for every new batch of data samples. An extremely aggressive way to keep the model performance at the best would be to incrementally train with every new data point and add previous samples as the remainder of the batch. This approach is extremely computation intensive and also less rewarding. This approach of becoming ultra-real-time and incrementally training for every new sample instead of a batch is usually not recommended.

Such models, which are always learning as and when a new batch of data is available, are called online models. The most popular examples of online models can be seen on your phone. Features like predictive text and autocorrect improve dramatically over time. If you generally type in a specific style, say combining two languages or shortening few words or using slang and so on, you will notice that the mobile phone quite actively tends to adapt to your style. This happens purely because the phone's operating system in the background initiates the mechanism for online models to learn constantly and improve.

Delivering Your Model As an API

The best practice today in delivering your model as a service to a larger software stack is by delivering it as an API. This is extremely useful and effective, as it completely gets rid of the tech-stack requirements. Your model can easily collaborate between a diverse and complex set of components in a software ecosystem where you can worry less about the language or framework you used to develop the model. Often, when you develop an ML or DL model, the choices to deliver the model are solely driven by two simple points:

- Build the model in a language that the software engineer understands

or

- Use an API

While Python and Keras are almost universal in today's modern tech stack, we can still expect a few exceptions where this choice might not be an easy option to integrate. Therefore, we can always choose API as the preferred mode of deployment for a DL model and define the requirements for data and calling style of the API appropriately.

There are two extremely useful and easy-to-operate options for deploying your service as an API. You could either use Flask (a lightweight Python web framework) or Amazon Sagemaker (available on AWS). There are other options too, and I encourage you to explore them. There is an extremely well-written article on Keras Blogs on deploying your DL model using Flask.

You can explore more on this here: `https://blog.keras.io/` `building-a-simple-keras-deep-learning-rest-api.html`.

Also, you can explore how to deploy your model as an API using AWS Sagemaker in a few steps here: `https://docs.aws.amazon.com/` `sagemaker/latest/dg/how-it-works-hosting.html`.

Putting All the Pieces of the Puzzle Together

Well, to conclude, we can gather all these small components we learned in the last section and put them together into a simple (small) architecture as shown in the following figure.

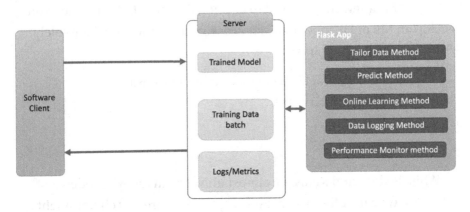

This is definitely an oversimplified explanation for producing your model; I recommend you to explore improved architectures for your use case in a more appropriate way. A ton of things will change the moment you have the scale, data volume, security, and availability at increased levels. The preceding visual showcases an architecture that works for small software. Once you are done with the model-building process, you can set up most of your logic to predict, tailor the data, measure performance periodically, automate online learning, logging, and so on into a small Flask app and run it on a server and deploy it as an API. The software client, which could be a web client or another service running on the same server, could leverage the model just by calling the API in the defined format. This architecture is okay for just small Proof of Concept (POC) and not recommended for production enterprise applications. Discussing large-scale deployment of DL models, the art of tailoring data on the fly, enabling online learning, and scaling the entire service would basically require a few more books.

Summary

In this chapter, we discussed the methods and strategies to look forward to when the model performance doesn't align with your expectations. In a nutshell, we studied the methods to incorporate when your DL model is not working well. We discussed regularization and hyperparameter tuning and also explored different strategies you could use to tune the hyperparameters and get an improved model. Lastly, we discussed a few principles we would need to address while deploying the model. We looked into an overview of the data-tailoring process for model prediction, understood how models can be trained using a pause-and-resume approach, and studied online models and the approaches to retrain them. Finally, we also looked at the options we can use to deploy the model and looked into a baby architecture for deploying the model using Flask.

CHAPTER 6

The Path Ahead

This fast-track introductory guide was designed to get you acquainted with the field of DL using Keras in the fastest yet most effective way. I hope you had a great time on this journey. In this final chapter, we will take a brief look at the path ahead. We will try to answer the following question: what additional topics are important for a data scientist to ace the DL journey?

Let's get started.

What's Next for DL Expertise?

We have covered the fundamentals in DL with DNNs for classification and regression. The most interesting part and in fact the major reason why DL gained its popularity and momentum in 2012 was DL for computer vision. A few years back, designing an algorithm that could help a computer in making sense out of an image was almost impossible. The idea of using algorithms to extract meanings from an image or classifying the image into a particular class was unimaginable. As time passed, ML became popular and the approach of using handcrafted features in images and then using a classifier for training the algorithm showcased improved results, but this was nowhere what we would want it to be. In 2012, Alexnet (an architecture developed by Alex Krizhevsky, Ilya Sutskever, and Geoffrey Hinton) was used to compete in the "ImageNet Large Scale Visual Recognition Challenge." This was a competition hosted for developing algorithms that could learn and predict on classifying images

© Jojo Moolayil 2019
J. Moolayil, *Learn Keras for Deep Neural Networks*,
https://doi.org/10.1007/978-1-4842-4240-7_6

into a defined set of classes. Alexnet achieved a top-five error of 15.3%; this was almost 11% lower than the previous best score and set a historic record in the challenge. The architecture was a type of DNN architecture especially used for image classification. That is when DL got noticed and immediately became a hot topic for research. The journey of DL from there onward skyrocketed. With more research and experiments on DL, the field got extended to video, audio, text, and pretty much any form of data. Today, DL is ubiquitous. Almost every major tech company has embraced DL in its entire stack of offerings.

A small step for you as a DL enthusiast in exploring advanced DL topics would be to first start with DL for computer vision. This is where you will explore convolutional neural networks (CNNs).

CNN

CNNs are the class of DL algorithms used for computer vision use cases like classifying an image or a video and detecting an object within an image or even a region within an image. CNN algorithms were a huge breakthrough in the field of computer vision, as it required a bare minimum of image processing compared to the other prevalent techniques of the time and also performed exceptionally well. The performance improvement with CNN for image classification was phenomenal. The process of building CNN is also simplified in Keras, where all the logical components are neatly abstracted. Keras provides CNN layers, and the overall process of developing CNN models is quite similar to what we learned while developing regression and classification models.

To give a brief understanding of the process, we will use a small example with its implementation. The following code snippet showcases a 'hello world' equivalent implementation for CNN. We will use the MNIST data (i.e., a collection of images with handwritten digits). The objective would be to classify the image as one of the digits from [0,1,2,3,4,5,6,7,8,9]. The data is already available in the Keras dataset module. Though the topic is entirely new, the comments within the code snippet will provide you with a basic idea of the model design.

```
#Importing the necessary packages
import numpy as np
import matplotlib.pyplot as plt
from keras.datasets import mnist
from keras.models import Sequential
from keras.layers import Dense, Dropout, Flatten
#Importing the CNN related layers as described in Chapter 2
from keras.layers.convolutional import Conv2D, MaxPooling2D
from keras.utils import np_utils

#Loading data from Keras datasets
(x_train, y_train), (x_test, y_test) = mnist.load_data()

#Defining the height and weight and number of samples
#Each Image is a 28 x 28 with 1 channel matrix
training_samples, height, width = x_train.shape
testing_samples,_,_ = x_test.shape

print("Training Samples:",training_samples)
print("Testing Samples:",testing_samples)
print("Height: "+str(height)+" x Width:"+ str(width))
```

Output

```
Training Samples: 60000
Testing Samples: 10000
Height: 28 x Width:28
```

The code continues:

```
#Lets have a look at a sample image in the training data
plt.imshow(x_train[0],cmap='gray', interpolation='none')
```

```
#We now have to engineer the image data into the right form
#For CNN, we would need the data in Height x Width X Channels
form Since the image is in grayscale, we will use channel = 1
channel =1
x_train = x_train.reshape(training_samples, height,
width,channel).astype('float32')
x_test = x_test.reshape(testing_samples, height, width,
channel).astype('float32')

#To improve the training process, we would need to standardize
or normalize the values We can achieve this using a simple
divide by 256 for all values
x_train = x_train/255
x_test =x_test/255

#Total number of digits  =10
target_classes = 10

# numbers 0-9, so ten classes
n_classes = 10

# convert integer labels into one-hot vectors
y_train = np_utils.to_categorical(y_train, n_classes)
y_test = np_utils.to_categorical(y_test, n_classes)

#Designing the CNN Model
model = Sequential()
model.add(Conv2D(64, (5, 5), input_shape=(height,width ,1),
activation='relu'))
model.add(MaxPooling2D(pool_size=(2, 2)))
model.add(Conv2D(64, (3, 3), activation='relu'))
model.add(MaxPooling2D(pool_size=(2, 2)))
```

```
model.add(Dropout(0.25))
model.add(Flatten())
model.add(Dense(128, activation='relu'))
model.add(Dense(n_classes, activation='softmax'))

# Compile model
model.compile(loss='categorical_crossentropy',
optimizer='adam', metrics=['accuracy'])

# Fit the model
model.fit(x_train, y_train, validation_data=(x_test, y_test),
epochs=10, batch_size=200)
```

Output

```
Train on 60000 samples, validate on 10000 samples
Epoch 1/10
60000/60000 [==============================] - 61s 1ms/step -
loss: 0.2452 - acc: 0.9266 - val_loss: 0.0627 - val_acc: 0.9806
Epoch 2/10
60000/60000 [==============================] - 64s 1ms/step -
loss: 0.0651 - acc: 0.9804 - val_loss: 0.0414 - val_acc: 0.9860
Epoch 3/10
60000/60000 [==============================] - 62s 1ms/step -
loss: 0.0457 - acc: 0.9858 - val_loss: 0.0274 - val_acc: 0.9912

 --- Skipping intermediate output----

Epoch 9/10
60000/60000 [==============================] - 58s 963us/step -
loss: 0.0172 - acc: 0.9943 - val_loss: 0.0284 - val_acc: 0.9904
Epoch 10/10
60000/60000 [==============================] - 56s 930us/step -
loss: 0.0149 - acc: 0.9949 - val_loss: 0.0204 - val_acc: 0.9936
```

Finally, let's evaluate the model performance:

```
metrics = model.evaluate(x_test, y_test, verbose=0)
for i in range(0,len(model.metrics_names)):
    print(str(model.metrics_names[i])+" = "+str(metrics[i]))
```

Output

```
loss = 0.02039033946258933
acc = 0.9936
```

We can see that we have an overall accuracy of ~99% on the test dataset. This was a rather simple example. Complications come in as and when the size of the image and the number of classes to predict increase.

To have a high-level understanding of how CNN works, you can refer to a couple of interesting blogs:

- https://adeshpande3.github.io/adeshpande3.
  github.io/A-Beginner's-Guide-To-Understanding-
  Convolutional-Neural-Networks/

- https://medium.freecodecamp.org/an-intuitive-
  guide-to-convolutional-neural-networks-
  260c2de0a050

To experiment more and study some really cool and simple-to-understand examples, you can check out a few popular git repositories for CNN-related use cases.

Here are a few:

- https://github.com/pranoyr/image-classification

- https://github.com/lrogar/distracted-driver-
  detection

RNN

The next step in DL after having explored CNN is to start exploring RNN, popularly known as "sequence models." This name became popular because RNN makes use of sequential information. So far, all the DNNs that we have explored process training data with the assumption that there is no relationship between any two training samples. However, this is an issue for many problems that we can solve using data. Consider the predictive text feature in your iOS or Android phone; the prediction of the next word is highly dependent on the last few words you already typed. That's where the sequential model comes into the picture. RNNs can also be understood as neural networks with memory. It connects a layer to itself and thereby gets simultaneous access to two or more consecutive input samples to process the end output. This property is unique to RNN, and with its rise in research, it delivered amazing success in the field of natural language understanding. All the legacy natural language processing techniques could now be significantly improved with RNNs. The rise of chatbots, improved autocorrect in text messaging, suggested reply in e-mail clients and other apps, and machine translation (i.e., translating text from a source language to a target language, Google Translate being the classic example) have all been propelled with the adoption of RNN. There are again different types of LSTM (long short-term memory) networks that overcome the limitations within the existing RNN architecture and take performance for natural language processing–related tasks a notch higher. The most popular versions of RNN are LSTM and GRU (gated recurrent unit) networks.

Similar to what we did for CNN, we will have a look at a simple (hello world equivalent) sample implementation for RNN/LSTM networks. The following code snippet performs a binary classification on the IMDB reviews dataset within Keras. It is a use case where we are provided with user reviews (text date) and an associated outcome as Positive or Negative.

```
#Import the necessary packages
from keras.datasets import imdb
from keras.models import Sequential
from keras.layers import Dense, LSTM
from keras.layers.embeddings import Embedding
from keras.preprocessing import sequence

#Setting a max cap for the number of distinct words
top_words = 5000
#Loading the training and test data from keras datasets
(x_train, y_train), (x_test, y_test) = imdb.load_data(num_
words=top_words)

#Since the length of each text will be varying
#We will pad the sequences (i.e. text) to get a uniform length
throughout
max_text_length = 500
x_train = sequence.pad_sequences(x_train, maxlen=max_text_
length)
x_test = sequence.pad_sequences(x_test, maxlen=max_text_length)

#Design the network
embedding_length = 32
model = Sequential()
model.add(Embedding(top_words, embedding_length, input_
length=max_text_length))
model.add(LSTM(100))
model.add(Dense(1, activation='sigmoid'))

#Compile the  model
model.compile(loss='binary_crossentropy', optimizer='adam',
metrics=['accuracy'])
```

```
#Fit the model
model.fit(x_train, y_train, validation_data=(x_test, y_test),
epochs=3, batch_size=64)
```

Output

```
Train on 25000 samples, validate on 25000 samples
Epoch 1/3
25000/25000 [==============================] - 222s 9ms/step -
loss: 0.5108 - acc: 0.7601 - val_loss: 0.3946 - val_acc: 0.8272
Epoch 2/3
25000/25000 [==============================] - 217s 9ms/step -
loss: 0.3241 - acc: 0.8707 - val_loss: 0.3489 - val_acc: 0.8517
Epoch 3/3
25000/25000 [==============================] - 214s 9ms/step -
loss: 0.3044 - acc: 0.8730 - val_loss: 0.5213 - val_acc: 0.7358
```

Evaluate the accuracy on the test dataset:

```
scores = model.evaluate(x_test, y_test, verbose=0)
print("Accuracy:",scores[1])
```

Output

```
Accuracy: 0.73584
```

The accuracy improved with an increased number of epochs for training and improved architectures. To get an overall understanding of how RNN works, you can explore a few blogs:

- https://colah.github.io/posts/2015-08-Understanding-LSTMs/

- https://medium.com/mlreview/understanding-lstm-and-its-diagrams-37e2f46f1714

- https://towardsdatascience.com/illustrated-
  guide-to-lstms-and-gru-s-a-step-by-step-
  explanation-44e9eb85bf21

To experiment more and study some really cool examples, you can check out a few popular git repositories for LSTM-related use case. Here are a few:

- https://github.com/philiparvidsson/LSTM-Text-
  Generation

- https://github.com/danielefranceschi/lstm-
  climatological-time-series

- https://github.com/shashankbhatt/Keras-LSTM-
  Sentiment-Classification

CNN + RNN

Another interesting area to explore within DL is the intersection of CNN and RNN. Sounds confusing? Just imagine you could combine the power of CNN (i.e., understanding images) and that of RNN (i.e., understanding natural text); what could the intersection or combination look like? You could describe a picture with words. That's right, by combining RNN and CNN together, we could help computers describe an image with natural-style text. The process is called image captioning. Today, if you search on google.com, a query like "yellow cars," your results will actually return a ton of yellow cars. If you imagine that the captioning for these images was done by humans, which could then be indexed by search engines, you are absolutely wrong. With humans, we can't scale the process of captioning images to billions of images per day. The process is simply not viable. You would need a smarter way to do that. Image captioning with CNN+RNN has brought a breakthrough not only in an image search for search engines but several other products we use in our day-to-day lives. The most important and revolutionary outcome that was delivered to mankind by the intersection of RNN and CNN was smart glasses (called duLight by Baidu): a camera equipped to reading glasses that could describe what the surroundings looked like. This was a great product for visually impaired people. Today, we have a smaller version of that implemented in a few apps that can be installed on the phone and works with the phone camera. If you are interested in reading more, you can explore the following blogs:

- `https://towardsdatascience.com/image-captioning-in-deep-learning-9cd23fb4d8d2`

- `https://machinelearningmastery.com/introduction-neural-machine-translation/`

- `https://towardsdatascience.com/neural-machine-translation-with-python-c2f0a34f7dd`

Showcasing examples of image captioning is out of the scope of this book. However, here are a few github repositories that you can start exploring:

- `https://github.com/yashk2810/Image-Captioning`

- `https://github.com/danieljl/keras-image-captioning`

Why Do We Need GPU for DL?

While exploring the environment set up in Chapter 2, we came across installing TensorFlow for GPU. I am sure you have already heard a lot about GPU being used for DL and companies like NVIDIA launching GPUs specially designed for DL. In general, the question anyone would first ask is what GPU has to do anything with DL. We'll try getting answers to this and other questions right away.

Given the exposure with DL you obtained in this guide, I presume you are already aware that DL is computationally intensive. It does take a lot of CPU power and time to get the models trained for a specific task. If you go one step deeper and try to understand what actually happens in a DL model's training process, it would boil down to one simple task (i.e., matrix multiplication). You have the input data in the form of a tensor (say, a three-dimensional matrix), the test data are in a similar form, the weights of the neuron connections are also stored in a matrix form, and in fact everything about a DNN of any form, say CNN, RNN, DNN, or the combination of all of them, are internally largely represented as matrices of different dimensions. The learning process with backpropagation also gets executed with matrix multiplication.

Interestingly, a large part of matrix multiplication can be processed in parallel. Therefore, to speed up the training process, the number of cores in your CPU can further improve the training time required for the model. Unfortunately, while the level of parallel processing achieved by CPUs is great, it's not the best. Especially for large matrix multiplication, the process is not as effective as we would want it to be.

However, we have GPUs that already available in the market. The primary purpose of using a GPU was for the enhanced video performance (i.e., higher screen refresh rate). In general, the screen of your laptop or computer is an image of a defined size, say 1920×1080 pixels. This image is again a three-dimensional matrix of the size $1920 \times 1080 \times 3$. The third dimension represents the color channel 'RGB'. So, in a nutshell, what you see on your screen at any point in time is an image displayed using a $1920 \times 1080 \times 3$ matrix. This matrix when refreshed (computed) 30 times a second becomes a smooth video, and you see the objects moving with no lag. So, to display something on the screen for just a second, the computer internally computes the values for the $1920 \times 1080 \times 3$ matrix at least 30 times. That's quite a lot of computation. Also, when you are playing games or performing any task that requires high-end graphics (tasks like video editing or designing images in Photoshop), the refresh rate needs a dramatic increment. A good estimate would be a screen refresh rate of 60 per second instead of 30. Now, to display this high graphic content there is an unusual extra load on the CPU and it might not be able to deliver the required performance. To solve this problem, we have GPUs that are specially designed for rendering high-end graphics by helping the computer in processing the computations required to refresh the screen 60 times. The GPU takes up the entire responsibility of processing the computation for screen refresh. This processing is done with massive parallel processing. The modern-day GPUs we use in a normal laptop would come with at least 400 cores, and the ones on the desktop are far more powerful. These cores help in massively parallel processing to display high-definition graphic content with high refresh rates.

It happens that the same tech can be embraced to solve the problems we face in DL. The massive parallel processing on matrices to render smooth graphic content on the screen can instead be used for processing the computation in the DL model's training process. In the wake of the moment, NVIDIA developed CUDA, which is a parallel processing interface model created for GPUs. It allows developers to use a CUDA-enabled graphics processing unit for general-purpose processing. This technology brought a huge breakthrough in training DL models. To describe it in numbers, a model that gets trained on my laptop on the CPU in 40 minutes gets trained within 2 minutes with the GPU. It is almost 20 times faster. You can imagine what we can achieve with even more powerful GPUs. Today, most DL libraries have support for GPUs. Once you install and set up the CUDA drivers for your GPU and install a GPU-compatible DL library, you are all set. The rest is completely abstracted for you. All you need to do is train the models the usual way and the framework takes care of seamlessly using resources from GPU as well as CPU.

The same process can also be achieved with GPUs from other manufacturers, like AMD with OpenGL. But NVIDAs GPUs are far superior and are at least five years ahead of any other competitor. If you are planning to invest in hardware for researching DL, I highly recommend buying a laptop or desktop (preferred) with an NVIDIA CUDA–compatible GPU. You will save a massive amount of time in your experiments.

Other Hot Areas in DL (GAN)

We explored the path forward for you to ace advanced DL topics. But this discussion would be incomplete without talking about the hottest areas for active research in DL. We will briefly talk about generative adversarial networks (GANs), though there are many more.

GANs are at the forefront of disruptions in DL and have been an active research topic recently. In a nutshell, a GAN allows a network to learn from images that represent a real-world entity (say, a cat or dog; when we simply develop a DL model to classify between a cat and a dog) and then generate a new image using the same features it has learned in the process; that is, it can generate a new image of a cat that looks (almost) authentic and is completely different from the set of images you provided for training. We can simplify the entire explanation for GAN into one simple task (i.e., image generation). If the training time and the sample images provided during train are sufficiently large, it can learn a network that can generate new images that are not identical to the ones you provided while training; it generates new images.

In case you are wondering about the applications of image generation, there are a whole new bunch of possibilities that had not been thought of until recently. Before, most DL models only Inference (relatively easy) and barely generated (very hard). If you look at the *Mona Lisa*, it is easy to classify it as a painting of a woman, but it would be really difficult to make one. If it were possible to do so, however, then a whole new generation of applications could be developed. To give you one great example, Indian online fashion retailer Myntra uses GAN to create new t-shirt designs. It trains a GAN network with a bunch of t-shirt designs and the model generates new designs. Out of 100 new designs generated by the system, even if 50 can be considered as good designs that they can manufacture, then the wonders in this field would be endless. The same idea can be extended to any other field. In the previous section, we talked about image captioning (i.e., generating natural text like descriptions from an image). That was already a cool application, now think about the reverse; think about providing a natural text description to a system and it generating a picture in return. The idea may sound too futuristic, but we are quite near to that possibility. Just imagine, you saw a criminal on the road and the police need your help in sketching his face to investigate further; with future GAN systems, we can imagine a system where you describe the details of the face of the criminal and the system sketches the face for you. The applications of GAN are too futuristic, but research is still in progress. As of now, GAN networks designed by researchers are able to render/generate images in high definition, and there are continuous experiments and research in the field to develop GAN networks that are capable of generating high-definition videos too.

You can read more about GAN and its applications here:

- https://medium.com/@awjuliani/generative-adversarial-networks-explained-with-a-classic-spongebob-squarepants-episode-54deab2fce39

- https://medium.com/ai-society/gans-from-scratch-1-a-deep-introduction-with-code-in-pytorch-and-tensorflow-cb03cdcdba0f

- https://towardsdatascience.com/understanding-generative-adversarial-networks-4dafc963f2ef

Concluding Thoughts

The agenda of this chapter was to highlight how promising the field of DL is and what a good time it is to start learning its foundations. I hope you now have a fair idea about the advanced topics in the field and the next steps you can take immediately to explore the DL frontier further. This book was designed to get you started in the fastest yet most effective way as an introductory guide to modern DL with DNNs.

We started this guide with a simple introduction to the topic of DL and understood its rationale and differences from the buzzwords in the market. We studied the necessity of using frameworks for developing DL models, explored a few popular choices in the market today, and understood why Keras has the strongest claim to be the preferred framework for a beginner. In later chapters, we explored the Keras framework by studying the logical abstractions it provides and mapping its equivalent in the DL ecosystem in small, incremental steps and then stitched together all the learnings with two foundational business-centric use cases in classification and regression. We then studied tips and tricks to design a network, a few workarounds in scenarios where getting started was difficult, and the process of model tuning with regularization and hyperparameter optimization. We also studied a few guidelines we should adhere to while deploying a DL model in production and finally took a sneak peek into the advanced offerings in DL with CNN, RNN, CNN+RNN, and the hottest research area in DL (i.e., GAN).

I thoroughly enjoyed the process of delivering the contents of this guide in an accelerated mode and I hope you enjoyed this journey too. With that, it is now time to sign off and wish you all phenomenal luck in your journey with DL. I wish you all a very happy and enjoyable learning path in developing your DL skills.

Index

A

Activation function, 24
Adaptive Moment Estimation
    (Adam), 37
Amazon Web Service Datasets, 54
Artificial intelligence (AI)
    ATM, 2
    definition, 2
    evolution, 53
    if-else rules, 2

B

Baseline accuracy, 118–119

C

Convolutional neural networks
    (CNNs), 162, 166, 170
CUDA-enabled graphics
    processing, 173

D, E, F

Data dictionary
    Assortment, 64
    CompetitionDistance, 64

CompetitionOpenSince
    [Month/Year], 64
Customers, 63
dataframes, 64–65
mainstream task, 66
Open, 63
Promo, 64
Promo2, 64
Promo2Since[Year/Week], 64
PromoInterval, 64
Sales, 63
SchoolHoliday, 63
StateHoliday, 63
Store, 63
StoreType, 64
unique method, 66
Data engineering
    Boolean columns, 110–111, 115
    categorical columns,
        111–112, 114
    data types, 110
    date-related features, 116
    date values, 112–113
    numeric feature, 114–115
    one-hot encoding, 115–116
    train, validation, and
        test, 117–118

Data exploration
  categorical features
    barplot function, 76–77
    seaborn package, 74–76
    StoreType and Assortment,
      74, 78
  data dictionary, 63–66
  data types, 66–67
  variable df, 61
  import pandas, 61
  Jupyter Notebooks, 61
  Kaggle, account registration, 60
  length and breadth,
      dataset, 61–63
  numeric columns, 70–74
  Python commands, 61
  sales prediction, 69–70
  store.csv, 62
  working with time, 67–69
Deep learning (DL), 21
  AI, 2, 5
  definition, 1
  frameworks
    building blocks, 9
    high-level, 11–12
    low-level, 9–11
    software industry, 8
    software tools, 8
    use cases, 9
  messaging system, 5
  ML, 2–5
  model performance and
      data size, 4

  neural network
    activation function, 6
    backpropagation, 7
    deep neural networks, 8
    hidden layers, 6
    input data, 6–7
    learning process in brain, 7
    logical building blocks, 6
    mathematical approach, 7
    message/signal passing, 5
    output of, 7
  social media, 5
  Venn diagram, 4
Deep neural network (DNN)
  activation function, 24
  building blocks, 45–46,
    48, 50, 52
  evaluation, 43–45
  input data, 21, 23
  layers, 28, 30, 32
  model configuration, 40
  models, 28
  neurons, 23
  ReLU function, 26–28
  training, 40–43
Designing DNN
  classification
    binary_crossentropy,
      119–120
    deeper network, 121–122
    medium-sized network,
      123–124
    number of neurons, 121

training process, 119
validation datasets, 121
coding, 86–88
computing power and time, 85
increasing neurons, 93–96
larger networks, 86
manual prediction, 98–99
model performance
improving, 89–93
testing, 89
optimization technique, 88
revisiting data, 86
small architectures, 85
training and validation loss,
epochs, 97–98
Dropout regularization
mechanism, 141–142

Keras, 12
Lasagne, 12
second level of abstraction, 11
Hyperparameter tuning
approaches
grid search, 148–151
manual search, 148
random search, 151
DL model
activation function, 147
batch size, 146
epochs, 145
learning rate, 146–147
number of neurons, 143–144
number of layers, 144–145
optimization, 147
weight initialization, 145–146

G

Gated recurrent unit (GRU), 167
Generative adversarial networks
(GANs), 174
Gluon, 12
Google Dataset Search, 54–55
GPUs, 171–173
Grid search, 148–151

H

High-level DL frameworks
first level of abstraction, 11
Gluon, 12

I, J

Indian Government Open Data, 54

K

Kaggle, 54–55
Keras framework
building, neural network, 14
data, 15
DNN, 13
dummy training dataset, 15
model structure, 15
trained model and predictions,
15–16

L

Lasagne, 12
Long short-term memory (LSTM)
    networks, 167
Loss function, 32–34
Low-level DL frameworks
    MxNet, 10
    PyTorch, 10
    TensorFlow, 11
    Theano, 9
    Torch, 10

M

Machine learning (ML)
    data availability, 3
    definition, 2
    historical test results and
        student attributes, 3
    neural networks, 3
    performance, 3
    statistical models, 4
    unstructured data types, 3
Mean absolute error (MAE), 84, 90
Metrics, 39
Minmaxscaler, 124
Model-building process, 158
Model deployment
    delivering API, 157–158
    online models, 156–157
    retraining, 155–156
    saving models to memory,
        154–155

    test data, 152–153
Model evaluation, 43–45
Model training, 40–43
Montreal Institute for Learning
    Algorithms (MILA), 9
MxNet, 10

N

Numeric columns
    clustering, 73
    CompetitionDistance, 73
    customers, 71
    hist function, 70
    histogram, 70–71
    isnull() command, 72, 73
    missing data points, 73
    Promo2, 71
    Promo2SinceWeek and
        Promo2SinceYear, 72
    replacing nulls with
        mode, 73

O

Online models, 156
Optimization
    algorithm, 147
Optimizers, 35–36
    Adam, 37
    SGD, 37
    techniques, 39
Overfitting, 137–139

P, Q

Pause-and-resume
approach, 156
Python
installation in Windows, Linux
and macOS, 18
TensorFlow, 17, 19, 21
versions, 17
PyTorch, 10

R

Rectified linear unit
(ReLU), 26
Recurrent neural network
(RNN), 31, 167, 169–170
Red Hat Business Value
archived competition, 101
baseline accuracy, 118–119
data engineering (*see* Data
engineering)
data exploration
activity data, 108
consolidate activity and
customer attributes
dataset, 109
customer activity, 106
download, datasets, 104
Jupyter Notebooks, 104
missing data points, 107
null values, 106
people dataset, 107

potential *vs.* nonpotential
customers, 109
train.csv, 106
training dataset, 105
download, 102
input data
standardization, 125–126
transformation, 126–127
medium-sized network,
127–129
problem statement
enterprise-grade
solutions, 102
high-value customers, 102
open source software
products, 102
potential customer, 104
SCQ, 103
training and validation
accuracy
epochs and predictions,
129–130
larger and deeper
network, 129
medium-sized deep
network, 130
model history and plots,
132–134
overfitting model, 134
test datasets, 130–132
Regularization, 139
L1, 140
L2, 140–141

Rossmann Store sales dataset
  data engineering and one-hot
      encoding
    contents, 82
    hardware resources, 80
    predictions, 84
    preprocessing module, 80
    Season, Store Type, and
      Assortment, 79
    shape command and data
      types, 81
    shapes, 83
    size of data, 79
    StateHoliday, 82
    training data, 79, 80
    train_test_split function,
      82–83
    train, validation, and test
      datasets, 82
  exploring data (*see* Data
    exploration)
  MAE, 84
  problem statement
    cross-sectional data, 59
    design principle, 56–57
    online data science
      competition, 56
    Rossmann, 55
    SCQ, 57–58

SCR, 56
stakeholder, 56
time-series forecasting
  problem, 59–60

S

Sigmoid function, 25
Situation Complication Question
  (SCQ), 57–58, 103
Situation–Complication–
  Resolution (SCR), 56
Standardscaler, 124
Stochastic gradient descent
  (SGD), 37

T

TensorFlow, 11–12, 19, 36
Tesla's cars, 5
Theano, 9
Time-series forecasting
  problem, 59–60
Torch, 10

U, V, W, X, Y, Z

UCI ML Repository, 55
US Government Open Data, 54

Printed in the United States
By Bookmasters